Module 1

Ayurvedic Dermatology Healing Skin from the Root

(30 Chapters)

DR MUKESH AGGARWAL

INDEX

PREFACE

In a world where modern dermatology often focuses on symptoms, Ayurveda invites us to look deeper — to the root of every imbalance. This is not just a philosophy but a lived science, practiced and preserved for millennia. Ayurderma – our 4-module course on Ayurvedic Dermatology, Trichology & Cosmetology – is born from the need to blend this timeless wisdom with today's clinical demands.

Module 1: Ayurvedic Dermatology – Healing Skin from the Root is the foundation stone of this journey. Through 30 carefully structured chapters, this book takes you through the profound understanding of skin health from the Ayurvedic perspective — not just as an organ, but as a mirror of inner harmony.

You will discover how the Tridoshas govern skin function, how Sapta Dhatus and Malas support vitality, and how classical concepts like Vicharchika, Kitibha, and Dadru are approached with holistic precision. The text goes beyond theory — you'll explore powerful herbs, formulation techniques, clinical case studies, and cleansing protocols grounded in both ancient scriptures and current clinical relevance.

Whether you're a seasoned Ayurvedic practitioner, a modern cosmetologist, or a medical student seeking integrative solutions, this module will help you connect the dots between tradition and transformation. We've also included Prakriti analysis, Trividha Pariksha, taila and lepa preparation methods, and practical applications for everyday skin conditions — empowering you to personalize care and cultivate lasting results.

By the end of this module, you won't just "know" Ayurvedic dermatology — you will feel it, apply it, and witness its power in practice.

- Module 2: Ayurvedic Trichology – Restoring Crowns with Herbs and Hands

In this module, we explore how Ayurveda sees the hair as an upadhatu (secondary tissue) of bone — and what that means for regrowth, reversal, and radiance.

- Module 3: Ayurvedic Cosmetology – Timeless Beauty from Within

This module is a treasure chest of Ayurvedic beauty rituals, ancient formulations, bridal protocols, and anti-aging secrets — all grounded in shastra and validated by modern science.

- Module 4: Practice Building & Clinical Integration – From Learner to Leader

This final section helps you translate wisdom into real-world clinical success. Learn how to design your practice, blend Ayurveda with cosmetology tools, and build a career with integrity.

Welcome to Ayurderma. Welcome to the ancient art of healing skin from the inside out.

Regards
Dr Mukesh Aggarwal
Founder, VHCA Hair Clinic

Chapter 1

INTRODUCTION TO AYURVEDIC DERMATOLOGY

FROM SHASTRA TO SKIN – THE JOURNEY OF AYURVEDIC HEALING

The Skin: A Mirror of Your Internal Cosmos

In Ayurveda, the skin is not just an outer covering—it is a darpaṇa (mirror) of your inner balance. Where modern medicine sees the skin as a protective organ, Ayurveda sees it as a reflection of your prakriti (constitution), ahara (diet), vihara (lifestyle), and manas (mind).

शरीरेन्द्रियसत्त्वात्मा संयोगो धर्म हेतवः।
"The union of body, senses, mind, and soul forms the foundation of health." – Charaka Samhita

Dermatological concerns are rarely skin-deep. Eczema, acne, psoriasis, fungal infections, pigmentation—these are all the outward signs of deeper disharmony between your doshas (Vata, Pitta, Kapha), dhatus (tissues), and agni (digestive fire).

The Need for Ayurvedic Dermatology Today

According to the WHO, 1 in 3 people globally suffer from a skin disorder at any given time. The rise of urban lifestyles, fast food, late nights, synthetic cosmetics, and chronic stress has led to an explosion of skin conditions.

Yet despite the advanced technology in dermatology, chronic skin diseases like eczema and psoriasis still lack permanent cures. This is where Ayurvedic dermatology offers a time-tested, holistic alternative.

Where allopathy suppresses symptoms, Ayurveda seeks samprapti vighatana—to break the chain of disease formation.

What is Ayurvedic Dermatology?

Ayurvedic Dermatology (Tvak Roga Chikitsa) is the branch of Ayurveda that focuses on diagnosing and treating skin diseases using principles of:

Tridosha balance
Shodhana (detoxification)
Shamana (palliation)
Rasayana (rejuvenation)
Dinacharya (daily routines)
Aahara-Vihara (diet and lifestyle)

Herbal formulations: lepa, taila, churna, kwatha, ghrita

It incorporates in-depth diagnostics like nadi pariksha (pulse reading), prakriti analysis, and trividha pariksha (inspection, palpation, questioning), which help personalize treatments.

A Holistic View of Skin

Ayurveda teaches us that the skin (tvak) is the seat of Sparshanendriya—the sense of touch, and is nourished by the rasa and rakta dhatus. Any disease of the skin, therefore, has both internal and external causes, such as:

Improper digestion (agnimandya)
Blood impurities (rakta dushti)
Emotional stress (manas vikara)
Toxin accumulation (ama)
Seasonal imbalance (ritu sandhi)
Wrong combinations of food (viruddha ahara)

Classical Classifications of Skin Diseases

Ayurvedic texts classify skin diseases under the term Kustha—a broad category encompassing 18 types of skin conditions, each associated with specific doshic imbalances.

These are further divided into:

Mahakustha – major skin diseases (e.g., psoriasis, leprosy)
Kshudra kustha – minor ones (e.g., acne, eczema)

This classical understanding, coupled with modern insights, forms the integrated approach you'll discover throughout this course.

A Modern Ayurvedic Dermatologist

An Ayurvedic dermatologist is more than a skin healer—they are a:

Dosha detective: identifying imbalances through observation and pulse
Herbal pharmacist: preparing customized formulations
Diet coach: correcting root causes through food
Mind therapist: addressing emotional toxins
Skin artist: restoring radiance holistically

What You'll Learn in This Module

This first module introduces you to 30 critical chapters covering the full spectrum of Ayurvedic skin care—from anatomy, diagnosis, classical conditions, and formulations to lifestyle, seasonal regimens, and patient case studies.

By the end, you'll be equipped to:

Diagnose skin diseases through Ayurvedic principles
Understand and manage common conditions like acne, eczema, pigmentation
Prepare and prescribe lepas, oils, and internal medicines
Guide patients with tailored diet and lifestyle changes
Document, consult, and treat real clinical cases
Your next patient awaits – with hope, with trust, and with falling hair. Be ready.

Your next patient awaits – with hope, with trust, and with falling hair. Be ready.

Conclusion:

Skin is sacred in Ayurveda—it is the outermost reflection of our innermost truth. This journey into Ayurvedic dermatology is more than academic—it is a sadhana, a sacred practice.

"Rogastu Dosha Vaishamyam, Arogya Dosha Samyam"
"Disease is caused by doshic imbalance; health is the harmony of doshas."

Let us now begin this healing journey—from roots to radiance.

Chapter 2

ANATOMY OF SKIN – AYURVEDIC VS. MODERN

“WHERE SCIENCE ENDS, AYURVEDA BEGINS”

त्वचा – देह का दरपन, आयुर्वेद का गहन विज्ञान

"त्वगादीनि च प्रत्यंगानि"
– Sushruta Samhita
(“Skin and its components are vital to understanding the whole body.”)

Modern dermatology sees the skin as a three-layered organ — epidermis, dermis, and subcutaneous tissue. But Ayurveda, thousands of years ago, spoke of 7 layers (tvacha ke sapta avaran), each with specific depth, functions, and diseases associated with it. This isn't mythology—this is metaphysical medicine backed by clinical observation.

Modern View: The Physiology of Skin

In modern science, skin is the largest organ, covering about 1.8 square meters, and weighing approximately 16% of total body weight. It serves as:

A barrier against infection and chemicals
A regulator of temperature and hydration
A sensor for touch, pain, and pressure
A communicator of emotions (blushing, sweating)
A producer of Vitamin D in sunlight

Each of the three layers has its own function:
Epidermis: Surface layer, constantly regenerating
Dermis: Rich in collagen, glands, follicles, vessels
Hypodermis: Fat cells for insulation and cushioning

But while these details help us understand the structure, they don’t explain why someone gets chronic eczema or adult acne, or how their emotions, digestion, and doshas interplay.

Ayurvedic Insight: The 7 Layers of Skin

"त्वचा सप्तधातुजा ज्ञेया सप्त त्वचां निवेशनात्।"
– Ashtanga Hridayam, Uttara Tantra
"The skin is born from all seven dhatus and is structured in seven layers."

Ayurveda reveals that skin is derived from all seven tissues (rasa, rakta, mamsa, meda, asthi, majja, shukra). Each layer is associated with a specific depth, vulnerability, and disease. Here's a poetic summary:

Avabhasini – The outermost layer, radiance-giving
Lohita – Governs complexion and pigmentation
Shweta – Associated with fairness and texture
Tamra – Seat of allergic and vascular reactions
Vedini – Linked to sensation and neural response
Rohini – Regeneration and healing
Mamsadhara – Deep anchoring of skin to muscle

Each of these layers is nourished by the dhatus, especially rasa and rakta. Any disturbance in their quality or flow leads to visible or invisible skin disorders.

Dual Perspective: Where They Meet

Where modern science studies skin as an organ, Ayurveda studies skin as a dynamic reflection of internal harmony.

Modern science provides depth, structure, and microscopic clarity.

Ayurveda provides wholeness, doshic influence, and systemic context.

Example:
Psoriasis is seen as autoimmune and inflammatory in modern medicine. Ayurveda explains it as kaphaja-kushtha with rakta dushti and ama accumulation—treatable with shodhana, shamana, and rasayana.

Clinical Correlation

Research shows that over 60% of chronic skin conditions show gut-related symptoms—constipation, indigestion, or acid reflux—proving Ayurveda's claim that skin health begins in the gut (agni).

"रोगाः सर्वे अपि मन्दे अग्नौ"
– Charaka Samhita
"All diseases begin with weak digestion."

So, while modern anatomy dissects, Ayurveda connects.

Ayurvedic Diagnostic Relevance
Understanding these seven layers helps a practitioner to:
Choose the right depth for lepa or taila application
Design a personalized dosha-specific skin care regimen
Select raktashodhaka or raktaprasadana herbs appropriately
Recommend internal rasayana therapy according to affected dhatus
Offer emotional counseling, as the vedini layer is linked to sensitivity and manas

Real-World Application
A patient with chronic dark patches may be diagnosed with melasma in modern terms, affecting the epidermis and basal melanocytes. But in Ayurveda, this points to the Lohita layer with pitta-rakta dushti, indicating the need for blood purification, cooling herbs, and anti-pitta diet.

A Holistic Vision
Skin is not just a layer—it is a language. Every spot, patch, itch, or lesion is a syllable of your inner story. The Ayurvedic dermatologist doesn't just treat symptoms—they translate this story and restore harmony.

"यथा पिंडे तथा ब्रह्मांडे"
"As in the microcosm, so in the macrocosm."

Conclusion:

Understand modern skin structure (epidermis, dermis, hypodermis)

Appreciate Ayurvedic view of 7 layers and their disease relevance

Begin viewing skin not as a surface but as a symptom of the soul

Prepare to correlate layers, doshas, and dhatus in diagnosis

Chapter 3

THE ROLE OF TRIDOSHA IN SKIN HEALTH

"DOṢA HI KĀRAṆAM ROGAṆĀM" – THE DOSHAS ARE THE ROOT CAUSE OF ALL DISEASES.

त्वचा: दोषों की दर्पण

The skin, though external in appearance, is the mirror of internal balance. Ayurveda asserts that every skin condition—from simple dryness to chronic eczema—is rooted in the vitiation of Vata, Pitta, and Kapha doshas. These bioenergetic forces regulate all bodily functions—including how your skin breathes, glows, reacts, and heals.

"वायुः पित्तं कफश्चैव त्रयो दोषाः समासतः। विकृताविकृताः देहे सर्वे रोगाः तु ते कारणम्॥"
– Charaka Samhita
(Vata, Pitta, and Kapha—when balanced, they sustain life; when imbalanced, they are the root of all diseases.)

Pitta: The Fiery Artist of Your Skin

Pitta dosha governs metabolism, heat, complexion, luster, and transformation. It resides mainly in rakta dhatu (blood) and skin tissues.

Balanced Pitta leads to:
- Radiant, glowing skin
- Healthy pigmentation
- Quick wound healing

Vitiated Pitta causes:
- Redness, burning, rashes, acne
- Psoriasis, eczema flares, urticaria
- Hyperpigmentation and inflammation

Stat: Nearly 80% of acute inflammatory skin diseases are linked to a Pitta imbalance due to modern lifestyle triggers: spicy food, alcohol, heat exposure, and stress.

"पित्तलानि विकारा स्युः रक्तगातानि सर्वशः।"
– Ashtanga Hridaya
(Pitta vitiates blood and causes inflammatory disorders.)

Vata: The Dry, Cracking Force
Vata dosha, composed of air and ether, is responsible for movement, dryness, roughness, and nerve conduction. It is deeply connected with touch, aging, and sensitivity of the skin.

Balanced Vata gives:
- Soft, supple skin
- Good sensory response
- Proper exfoliation and elasticity

Vitiated Vata leads to:
- Dry, flaky, cracked skin
- Wrinkles, premature aging
- Eczema with dryness, itchiness, discoloration

Clinical Insight: Most aging-related skin concerns (like fine lines and cracks) are strongly linked to elevated Vata and depleted rasa dhatu.

Kapha: The Moisturizer and Protector

Kapha dosha offers structure, moisture, stability, and immunity to the skin. It nourishes the dermal layers and provides the skin with its natural hydration and coolness.

Balanced Kapha grants:
- Smooth, moisturized skin
- Resistance to external allergens
- Slow, graceful aging

Vitiated Kapha results in:
- Oily, sticky skin
- Cystic acne, boils, comedones
- Fungal infections, sluggish wound healing

Clinical Pattern: In patients with seborrheic dermatitis, malassezia overgrowth is aggravated by kapha dominance, poor hygiene, and undigested toxins (āma).

"कफस्त्वचां स्निग्धता कारणं भवति।"
(Kapha is responsible for the smoothness and oiliness of the skin.)

Doshas & Skin Conditions: Clinical Correlations

Skin ConditionDominant DoshaAyurvedic TermEczema (Dry)VataVicharchika (Vata-dominant)PsoriasisVata + KaphaKitibhaAcne (Inflammatory)PittaYuvan PidikaOily Skin & PimplesKaphaKaphaja PidikaPigmentation, MelasmaPitta + Rakta DushtiNeelika / VyangaFungal InfectionsKapha + VataDadru

Skin as a Dosha Canvas

Your skin tells your dosha story every day:
- Does it blush easily? Pitta
- Does it flake in winter? Vata
- Does it feel sticky and break out? Kapha

Ayurvedic dermatology empowers you to go beyond external treatments and work on internal corrections. No steroid cream can balance a dosha. But a tridosha-based approach ensures the root is healed.

Managing Dosha Imbalances

For Pitta Skin Issues:
- Cool herbs: Manjishtha, Neem, Sariva
- Panchakarma: Virechana, Rakta Moksha
- Diet: Avoid spicy, sour, fermented foods

For Vata Skin Issues:
- Oils: Bala Taila, Kumari Taila, Ashwagandha Taila
- Abhyanga with warm oils
- Diet: Ghee, warm moist foods, no fasting

For Kapha Skin Issues:

- Herbs: Haridra, Triphala, Daruharidra
- Ubtans with mustard or tulsi
- Diet: Dry, warm, light food; less sugar

Conclusion:

Skin doesn't lie. Every rash speaks your Pitta, every crack your Vata, and every oil-slick your Kapha. A good Ayurvedic dermatologist is a dosha detective who reads this map and prescribes not creams, but constitutional change.

"सर्वे दोषाः त्वचां स्पृशन्ति।"
– Charaka Samhita
(All doshas affect the skin—diagnose the dominant one, treat the root.)

Chapter 4

SAPTA DHATU & MALAS – FOUNDATION OF SKIN VITALITY

HĀTUMĀLYAMARUTPITTAŚLEṢMAṆĀṂ SĀMYAM ĀROGYAṂ VIPARYAYO VIKĀRAḤ I"— CHARAKA SAMHITA

त्वचा का निर्माण – भीतर की परतों से बाहर की आभा तक

What we see on the surface—clear, radiant, or blemished skin—is merely the final reflection of a deep internal architecture. Ayurveda reveals that the skin is not just a layer, it is the expression of seven dhatus (body tissues) and the proper excretion of malas (wastes).

If these dhatus are nourished and their malas excreted properly, the skin naturally becomes healthy, glowing, and disease-resistant. But any disruption at any layer leads to the manifestation of twak vikara (skin disorders).

The Seven Tissues – The Skin's Hidden Architects

Let's journey through the seven dhatus and understand how each plays a pivotal role in skin vitality.

Rasa Dhatu (Plasma/Lymph):
- First product of digestion.
- Circulates nutrition to skin.
- Deficiency → Dryness, dullness, lack of glow.

Rakta Dhatu (Blood):
- The foundation of complexion and vitality.
- Directly nourishes the skin and is closely linked with Pitta dosha.
- Impurity → Redness, boils, rashes, acne, pigmentation.

"रक्तं त्वचां पातीति" – रक्त ही त्वचा का पोषक है।

Mamsa Dhatu (Muscle Tissue):
- Gives firmness and structure to skin.

- Supports hair follicles and sebaceous glands.
- Deficiency → Loose, sagging skin or weak hair root bed.

Meda Dhatu (Adipose/Fat):
- Provides softness and oiliness.
- Acts as a natural skin moisturizer.
- Excess → Oily skin, cystic acne; Deficiency → Dry, undernourished skin.

Asthi Dhatu (Bones):
- Though hidden, it governs nails, hair and deeper firmness.
- Imbalance → Brittle nails, hair fall, early wrinkles.

Majja Dhatu (Bone Marrow & Nervous Tissue):
- Supports neuro-cutaneous pathways.
- Enhances skin response to temperature, pressure, pain.
- Deficiency → Lack of glow, sensory disturbances in skin.

Shukra Dhatu (Reproductive Essence):
- The most refined dhatu.
- Responsible for Ojas—the glow, strength, and immunity of skin.
- Low Ojas → Lusterless, aged, lifeless skin.

Statistically Speaking

Modern dermatology recognizes how collagen (mamsa), lipid layers (meda), blood vessels (rakta), and nerves (majja) contribute to skin quality. Ayurveda recognized this over 3,000 years ago. For instance:

Over 70% of chronic skin disorders are related to rakta and rasa vitiation.

Hormonal issues (linked with shukra and meda dhatu) are major causes of adult acne and pigmentation.

Malas: The Waste Management System

Just like a beautiful house needs good drainage, your skin needs clean elimination of waste.
There are three primary malas that impact skin health:

Purisha (Stool):
- Constipation → Toxin buildup → Skin dullness, acne, itching.

Mutra (Urine):
- Removes fluidic waste and heat.
- Excess heat → Pitta skin issues (burning, redness, boils).

Sveda (Sweat):
- Directly excreted through skin.
- Blocked sveda → Heat rashes, body odor, fungal infections.
- Excess → Sticky skin, Kapha accumulation, seborrhea.

"सर्वे दोषाः मलानां विघातात् विकारं कुर्वन्ति।"
(When malas are not excreted properly, doshas get aggravated and cause disease.)

Clinical Perspective

A young woman with acne and irregular periods has:
- Impaired rasa & rakta dhatus → acne
- Malfunctioning shukra & meda dhatu → hormonal imbalance
- Constipation → āma → toxin accumulation in skin

Rather than prescribing creams, Ayurveda would suggest:
- Raktashodhak herbs (Manjistha, Neem, Sariva)
- Virechana for Pitta
- Abhyanga + swedana to clear malas
- Diet tailored to clean rasa and enhance agni

From Layers to Luminance

Healthy skin is not applied, it is cultivated from within. Each dhatu nourishes the next like a relay race:

Rasa → Rakta → Mamsa → Meda → Asthi → Majja → Shukra → Ojas → Glow.

If the link is broken at any point, the result is vikriti – imbalance that reflects on your skin.

"ओजो हि परमो धातुः" – ओजस ही संपूर्ण सौंदर्य का सार है।

Conclusion:

- Nourish your dhatus through proper digestion, herbs, and lifestyle.
- Support malas with panchakarma, regular bowel habits, hydration, and cleansing herbs.
- Remember, skin health is not cosmetic—it's constitutional.

Chapter 5

KUSTHA – CLASSIFICATION OF SKIN DISORDERS

"कुष्ठं नाम चिरं रोगं स्रंसनं रौक्षणं तथा।
दोषाणामुपशान्तानां पुनर्लक्ष्मं प्रदर्शयेत्॥"
— Charaka Samhita, Chikitsa Sthana

क्यों कहते हैं आयुर्वेद में त्वचा रोग को 'कुष्ठ' ?

In Ayurveda, all chronic skin diseases fall under the broader term "Kustha", not because they are contagious, but because they deeply affect the skin, tissues, and sometimes the mind. The term "कुष्ठ" itself signifies a disfiguring, long-lasting and dosha-deep-rooted disease. Unlike modern dermatology which classifies diseases based on pathology or microbiology, Ayurveda classifies them holistically—based on dosha, dushya, dhatu, srotas, and manas.

A Statistical Reality

Over 1 in 10 people in India suffer from chronic skin issues.

WHO estimates that over 30% of global dermatological issues are unresolved by modern treatment.

Ayurvedic classics classify 18 types of Kustha, offering personalized solutions, while modern dermatology often limits itself to symptomatic treatment.

Kustha – A Precise Ayurvedic Classification

Charaka, Sushruta, and Vagbhata unanimously describe two categories of skin disorders:
Mahakustha (Major types) and Kshudra Kustha (Minor types).
This division is based on dosha predominance, severity, dhatu involvement, prognosis, and deformity risk.

महाकुष्ठ (Major Skin Disorders – 7 types)
These are severe, stubborn, and deeply rooted diseases, often affecting multiple dhatus and involving deformity or recurrence.

Some examples include:

Kapala Kustha – Thickened, scaly skin (resembles Psoriasis)
Audumbara Kustha – Reddish eruptions with burning (like Dermatitis)
Rishyajihva Kustha – Skin with cracks and splits (like Ichthyosis)
Pundarika Kustha – White, scaly patches (akin to Leucoderma)
Daruna Kustha – Dry, painful, thick skin (eczema-like)
Arunshika Kustha – Boil-like eruptions
Kakana Kustha – Extremely painful, ulcerative lesions
These are usually tridoshaja in nature and require combined shodhana (purification) and shamana (pacifying) therapies.

क्षुद्र कुष्ठ (Minor Skin Disorders – 11 types)

These are less severe, superficial and easier to treat, usually involving only one or two doshas. Examples include:

Vicharchika – Eczema
Dadru – Fungal Ringworm
Kitibha – Psoriasis
Charmadala – Dermatitis with itching
Pama – Scabies-like eruptions
Alasa – Oozing lesions
Vipadika – Cracked soles
Shvitra – Leucoderma
Kakunaka – Pustular lesions
Kusthaku – Sebaceous gland issues

These may not cause gross deformity but can be stubborn or recurrent if not treated according to dosha-dushya-srotas.

The Dosha Blueprint of Kustha

"सर्वं कुष्ठं त्रिदोषजं।"
(All skin disorders have tridoshic origin.)

However, each disorder shows dosha dominance, which is crucial for correct chikitsa:

Vata-dominant Kustha → Dryness, blackish color, cracks
Pitta-dominant Kustha → Redness, burning, pus, heat
Kapha-dominant Kustha → Oiliness, thick skin, white scaling, itching

By observing color, discharge, itch, pain, and patch shape, an Ayurvedic physician determines the exact dosha pattern, leading to precision treatment.

Case Example: Vicharchika (Eczema)

A patient presents with dry, red patches that itch and ooze. Ayurveda classifies this under Vicharchika—a kapha-pitta dominant kshudra kustha.
Modern diagnosis may simply call it eczema and give steroids, but Ayurveda looks deeper:
- Kapha: oozing, heaviness
- Pitta: redness, burning
- Vata (if chronic): dryness, scaling

Treatment includes:
- Virechana to detoxify pitta
- Herbs like Khadira, Nimba, Manjistha
- Taila lepa with medicated oils
- Diet restrictions on curd, sour, fermented foods

Why Kustha is Not Just a Skin Issue

Ayurveda sees skin disorders as a reflection of deeper mala sanchaya (toxin accumulation), poor agni, and mental stress.

"मानसिक दोषाः अपि त्वचा विकारं जनयन्ति।"
(Mental disturbances also lead to skin disorders.)

Thus, treatment isn't just topical but holistic:
- Internal purification
- Rasayana for immunity
- Stress management (Manas Shanti)
- Lifestyle and food corrections

Integration with Modern Medicine

Ayurveda can successfully treat psoriasis, eczema, acne, fungal infections, and leucoderma with internal & external herbs, panchakarma, and diet.

Studies have shown that Khadirarishta and Panchtikta Ghrita are effective in autoimmune skin conditions.

Panchakarma has shown over 60% improvement in chronic skin diseases in recent AYUSH trials.

Conclusion:

- All skin disorders fall under "Kustha" but are classified with great precision
- Dosha analysis is the core of diagnosis and treatment
- Even the "minor" skin disorders can become "major" if neglected
- Kustha reflects internal metabolic and emotional imbalances
- Holistic, not cosmetic, healing is the Ayurvedic path

In the next chapter, we'll explore Vicharchika (Eczema) in detail, its causes, doshic patterns, symptoms, and step-by-step Ayurvedic chikitsa.

Let's uncover how Ayurveda doesn't suppress but eliminates skin disease from its roots.

Chapter 6

UNDERSTANDING VICHARCHIKA (ECZEMA)

An Ayurvedic Blueprint

"विचर्चिका त्वग्गतः पित्तकफप्रकोपजः।
कण्डू-पाका-रुजः-स्वेद-दाह-स्रावसमन्वितः॥"
— Charaka Samhita, Chikitsa Sthana

What is Vicharchika?

In modern terms, Eczema is described as an inflammatory skin condition, marked by itching, redness, oozing, scaling, and even cracking. But in Ayurveda, it is more than a skin disease—it is a reflection of internal doshic imbalance, particularly of Kapha and Pitta, combined with Rakta and Twacha dushti.

Vicharchika is not merely a skin irritation; it is a loud cry of the body for internal cleansing.

Modern Stats Meet Ancient Wisdom
Around 15–20% of children and 10% of adults suffer from some form of eczema globally.
Nearly 60% of cases are treated symptomatically with steroids, often leading to recurrence.
Ayurvedic texts describe Vicharchika as a stubborn, kaphaja-pittaja skin disorder with chronic tendencies and recurrence if not purified from the root.

Lakshana (Symptoms) of Vicharchika

Ayurveda describes specific signs that match modern eczema yet go beyond just what is visible:
Kandu (Itching) – Profound, often unbearable
Paka (Inflammation) – Reddish or blackish discoloration
Ruja (Pain) – Burning, aching sensation
Srav (Discharge) – Oozing, especially yellow or white
Pidika (Blisters) – Small eruptions or boils
Shyava Varna – Blackish hue on chronic lesions
Rukshata – Dryness, cracking

Doshic Involvement

"Vicharchika is predominantly a Kapha-Pitta disorder with secondary involvement of Vata and Rakta."

Kapha causes itching, heaviness, and discharge.
Pitta leads to inflammation, redness, and burning.
Vata when chronic causes dryness, scaling, and pain.
Rakta (blood tissue) is invariably affected, making raktashuddhi an essential treatment line.

Samprapti (Pathogenesis)

Agnimandya (weakened digestion) leads to production of ama (toxins).
Ama mixes with doshas—mainly Kapha and Pitta.
These vitiated doshas circulate and localize in twak (skin), rakta (blood), mamsa (muscle), lasika (lymph).
Manifestation of visible symptoms: itching, oozing, lesions, etc.
If left untreated, it becomes chronic and resistant.

Case Reflection

A 35-year-old woman reports dry, red, itchy patches on forearms and behind knees for 5 years. Modern diagnosis: Chronic Eczema. Treatment: Corticosteroids, with temporary relief.

Ayurvedic approach:

Kaphapittaja Vicharchika, involving Rakta Dushti
Advised Virechana (purgation) for Pitta
Internal herbs: Khadir, Manjistha, Haridra
Lepa (herbal paste) with Daruharidra and Nimba
Diet: Avoid fermented, sour, spicy food
Lifestyle: Daily Abhyanga with medicated oil + regular Vamana advised seasonally

Result: Visible improvement in 3 weeks, oozing stopped, itching reduced, and skin restored in 3 months with maintenance Rasayana.

Shamana Chikitsa (Palliative Therapy)

Internal Medicines:

Khadirarishta – for blood purification
Mahamanjishthadi Kwath – detoxifying and anti-inflammatory
Guggulu Tikta Ghrita – healing deep-seated toxins

External Applications:

Lepa of Haridra + Daruharidra + Chandana
Taila: Use of Jatyadi taila, Nalpamaradi taila
Raktamokshana (bloodletting) in chronic stubborn cases

Diet & Lifestyle:

Avoid curd, fried, sour, and fermented food
Regular sleep, mental calmness, skin hydration

Shodhana Chikitsa (Detox Therapy)

According to classics, shodhana is the most effective and long-lasting cure. The following are highly effective in Vicharchika:

Virechana – For Pitta dushti
Raktamokshana – For Rakta shuddhi
Vamana – If Kapha is dominant and itching is severe
Basti – For chronic or Vata involvement

Research Corner
A clinical trial at BHU using Khadira decoction and Manjistha capsules showed 72% improvement in chronic eczema within 8 weeks.

A 2022 AYUSH trial showed significant results in Vicharchika with Virechana + Tikta ghrita + Rasayana compared to only local application.

Practical Insights for Students & Practitioners

Never treat eczema as a skin-only disorder. Always check digestion, stress levels, bowel movements.

Educate the patient about recurrence if ama is not cleared.
Maintain photo documentation before, during, and after treatment.
Always start with dipana-pachana (digestive fire enhancement) before detox.
Recommend seasonal detox in chronic patients.

Manas Connection

Emotional factors like anxiety, suppressed anger, and frustration worsen eczema.

"मनः प्रसादः सौन्दर्यं वर्धयति।"
(Mental peace enhances beauty.)

Thus, incorporating pranayama, shirodhara, nasya, and counseling supports healing.

Conclusion:

Vicharchika is a Kapha-Pitta Rakta pradhana twak vikara

Root cause lies in ama, agnimandya, and dosha dushti

Requires a combination of shodhana, shamana, rasayana

Avoidance of nidana (causative factors) is as important as treatment

Mind-body balance, sattvic diet, and routine enhance recovery

Chapter 7

DADRU (RINGWORM) – PATHOGENESIS & PROTOCOL

"त्वग्गतः पित्तकफाभ्यां सम्प्राप्तो दद्रुरुच्यते।"
— Madhava Nidana

Introduction to Dadru in Ayurveda

Dadru, commonly identified today as Ringworm, is one of the most frequently encountered fungal skin infections. Unlike superficial treatment approaches that suppress the symptoms, Ayurveda delves into doshic roots, particularly Pitta and Kapha vitiation, and addresses the entire system.

Dadru is not just a skin affliction. It is a burning imbalance ignited by wrong food, bad hygiene, and an overheated inner fire (Pitta).

Samprapti (Pathogenesis)

According to Ayurvedic texts, Pittakaphaja dosha combine with Rakta and Twak dhatus, obstructing the proper flow of nutrients and heat. The result: itchy, circular, red, and burning eruptions.

"शीतोष्णभोजनं स्वप्नो दिवा, च कफ्हार्तिभुक्तं च यः सेवनात्।
दद्रुर्भवेत् त्वक्चमसंनिपातं, कण्डूर्दाहो रक्तवर्णं च लक्षणम्॥"
– Bhavaprakasha

Clinical Features of Dadru (Lakshana)
Kandu (intense itching)
Raga (reddish circular patches)
Pidaka (small raised eruptions)
Utsanna Mandala (elevated circular lesion)
Daha (burning sensation)
Shwet-Peet-Srav (white or yellowish discharge in chronic cases)
Krimija Lakshana (microbial origin recognized as Krimi)

Modern View & Epidemiology

WHO reports that nearly 20–25% of the global population suffers from some form of fungal skin infection at any time.
India has witnessed a 250% rise in chronic and steroid-resistant fungal infections in the past 5 years (ICMR, 2021).

Excessive use of creams like steroid combinations (e.g., clobetasol) has led to Tinea incognito, a hidden and resistant form of ringworm.

Nidana (Causative Factors)

Excessive consumption of curd, fish, milk with salt
Day sleeping, sedentary lifestyle
Use of tight, non-breathable clothing
Poor hygiene or shared towels, clothing
Stress, suppressed sweating, and lack of detox

These nidanas lead to ama production, disturbing Kapha and Pitta, and creating a perfect medium for krimija vikaras (fungal growth).

Ayurvedic Chikitsa (Treatment)

1. Shodhana (Detoxification):
Virechana – Clears Pitta from Rakta
Raktamokshana – In stubborn, chronic cases
Snehapana (ghee intake) with Tikta ghrita before Virechana

2. Shamana (Pacification Therapy):

Internal Medicines:
Arogyavardhini Vati
Panchtikta Ghrita Guggulu
Khadirarishta
Manjishthadi Kwath

External Application:

Lepa of Haridra, Daruharidra, Nimba, and Gandhak
Karanj Taila, Chandanaadi Taila for soothing
Dusting powders with Talc + Neem + Tankan

3. Dietary Guidelines (Pathya-Apathya):
Avoid:

Curd, sour items, fermented foods, excess ghee/oil

Embrace:

Bitter vegetables (Neem, Karela)
Barley, old rice, moong dal
Warm water, detox teas with Triphala + Giloy

Psychological Angle & Lifestyle

Ringworm thrives on stress and suppression. Mental irritation can aggravate Pitta, worsening symptoms.

"मनसः क्लेशात् दोषप्रकोपः स्यात्।"
(Mental distress leads to dosha imbalance.)

Hence, meditation, maintaining hygiene, regular abhyanga (oil massage) and daily snana (bathing) with herbal water (triphala, neem leaves) are crucial.

Research Insight

A study published in AYU Journal (2019) found that patients treated with Haridra Khanda and Khadir Kwath + Lepa showed over 70% recovery within 4 weeks, without recurrence for 6 months.

Another study conducted at Gujarat Ayurved University on Karanj Taila + Gandhak Rasayan showed remarkable improvement in fungal infections within 2 weeks.

Case Snapshot

A 17-year-old male had recurring ringworm over groin and back for 9 months. Previous steroid-antifungal creams gave temporary relief.

Ayurvedic Approach:

Nidana Parivarjana – Complete stoppage of curd, tight jeans, day sleep
Khadirarishta + Triphala Guggulu internally
Neem-Haridra Lepa externally
Virechana with Eranda Taila in 3rd week

Result: 85% improvement in 1 month; no recurrence at 3-month follow-up.

Key Ayurvedic Insights

Dadru is more than fungal—it is a dosha + dhatu dushti + krimi pathology.
Shodhana is essential in chronic or relapsing conditions.
Sattvic lifestyle, internal cleansing, and skin hygiene are non-negotiable pillars of therapy.
Recurrent cases are a sign of deep-seated Kapha-Pitta-Ama imbalance, needing holistic correction.

Spiritual Lens

In Ayurveda, skin represents the mirror of the inner fire and emotion. When Kapha (dampness) and Pitta (heat) collide, infections flourish.

"त्वचा हि शोभा जीवितस्य प्रतीका।"

Thus, skin health is a reflection of internal purity, peace, and balance.

Chapter 8

KITIBHA (PSORIASIS) AYURVEDIC LENS

"त्वचां विकारो बहुधा दृश्यते, तत्र किटिभं शुष्कत्वं रुक्षता च प्रमुखम्।"
— Charaka Samhita

Introduction to Kitibha

In Ayurveda, Kitibha is classified under Kustha (skin diseases) and often correlates clinically with Psoriasis, a chronic, immune-mediated, non-contagious skin disorder marked by scaling, itching, and thickened plaques.

Ayurveda perceives this not as an isolated skin anomaly, but a deeply systemic doshic disharmony, prominently involving Vata and Kapha, coupled with Rasa, Rakta, Mamsa, and Meda dhatu dushti.

"किटिभं नाम त्वग्गतः वातकफप्रकोपजं रुक्षं स्पर्शासहं च त्वचा विकारम्।"

Ayurvedic Pathogenesis (Samprapti)

Vata aggravation leads to dryness (rukshata), scaling (parushata), and pain.

Kapha contributes to thickness, itching (kandu), and sluggish dhatu metabolism.

Contaminated Rakta and Mamsa dhatu create chronic inflammation and skin cell overproduction.

The skin, when deprived of proper rasayana and dhatu nutrition, becomes a battleground for auto-reactivity, a term modern science uses to describe psoriasis.

Clinical Features (Lakshana of Kitibha)

Rukshata – Extreme dryness
Parushata – Roughness like tree bark

Kandu – Persistent itching
Shyava Varna – Discoloration (blackish-brown patches)
Utkledita Twacha – Thickened, raised skin lesions
Mandala – Well-defined circular lesions
Aswedanam – Absence of sweating from affected skin

"रुक्षा श्यावा कण्डुयुक्ता स्पर्शासहा च सा।
मण्डला किटिभा ज्ञेया त्वक्किकारेषु विश्रुता॥"
– Madhava Nidana

Modern Correlation & Statistics

Psoriasis affects 2–3% of the world population.
In India, prevalence ranges from 0.4% to 2.8%, most common in 30–50 age group.
40% of patients develop Psoriatic Arthritis over time.
Stress, climate, and genetics play a significant aggravating role.
Research reveals elevated levels of interleukin-17 and TNF-alpha, linking psoriasis with systemic inflammation—confirming Ayurvedic insight that it is not just skin-deep.

Nidana (Causative Factors)

Viruddha Ahara (e.g., fish + milk, curd + meat)
Heavy, oily, fermented, stale food
Sedentary lifestyle and excessive sleeping
Suppression of natural urges (vegavidharan)
Mental stress, unresolved grief, and emotional suppression
Accumulation of ama (toxins) in deeper tissues

Chikitsa Sutra – The Ayurvedic Approach

1. Shodhana Chikitsa (Purification Therapies)
Snehapana: Ghrita with Panchtikta or Mahatikta
Vamana: For Kapha dominant Kitibha
Virechana: For Pitta-Rakta clearance
Raktamokshana: Local bloodletting in plaque-rich zones
Basti Karma: Niruha with Tikta dravyas for chronic, systemic detox

2. Shamana Chikitsa (Pacification Treatment)

Internal Medications:

Panchtikta Ghrita Guggulu
Arogyavardhini Vati
Khadirarishta
Mahamanjishtadi Kwath
Gandhak Rasayan

External Therapies:

Tikta Lepa of Neem, Haridra, Manjishtha, Daruharidra
Oil application with Jatyadi Taila, Chandanaadi Taila
Takra Dhara (buttermilk dripping therapy) for severe itching
Udwartana (dry powder massage) in obese patients with Kitibha

Pathya-Apathya (Do's and Don'ts)

Favor:

Bitter vegetables (Neem, Giloy, Patola)
Barley, green gram, old rice
Detox teas, warm water, ghee in moderation
Meditation, pranayama, self-love therapy

Avoid:

Curd, fish, dairy + meat combinations
Cold foods, sweets, night awakening
Emotional suppression and anger

Case Insight

A 38-year-old female with plaque psoriasis over elbows and scalp for 4 years, under methotrexate with minimal relief.

Ayurvedic Plan:

Tikta Ghrita Snehapana (internal oleation)
Virechana with Trivrit + Draksha decoction
Internal meds: Gandhak Rasayan, Manjishthadi Kwath
External: Neem-Haridra Lepa + Chandana Taila

Result:
80% improvement in scaling and itching in 2 months. Emotional wellbeing also restored with Shirodhara.

Research Highlight

A study published in Journal of Research in Ayurveda (2020) demonstrated that Panchtikta Ghrita Guggulu + Virechana + Raktamokshan protocol led to complete remission in 63% of chronic psoriasis patients over 3 months.

Mind-Body Connection

Psoriasis flares are closely linked to mental trauma, suppressed rage, and unresolved fear. Vata dosha, being highly mobile and sensitive to thoughts, plays a pivotal role.

"मन एव कारणं बन्धमोक्षयोः।"
– Yoga Vasistha

Practices like meditation, affirmations, chanting, and Dinacharya align internal rhythms, calming both skin and soul.

Conclusion

Kitibha is not just a skin ailment—it is a call to detoxify, de-stress, and restore inner harmony. Ayurveda treats it through a comprehensive system of deep cleansing, dosha pacification, dhatu rejuvenation, and spiritual healing.

"When the skin peels, it is not just a disease leaving—it's a rebirth."

Chapter 9

TWAK VIKARA – COMMON SKIN IMBALANCES

"त्वचा दोषैः समुत्पन्ना विकाराः पञ्चभिः स्मृताः।
रागः, श्यावा, कण्डुः, रुक्षता, स्वेददोषश्च॥"
— Ashtanga Hridaya

Introduction: Skin—The Mirror of Inner Balance

Our skin (twak) is more than just a physical barrier. In Ayurveda, it is a reflective surface for internal balance (samya) or imbalance (vishama). When doshas are vitiated, they often manifest externally first—making twak vikara not merely cosmetic concerns but physiological alarms.

"The skin speaks what the gut and mind conceal."

Twak: An Ayurvedic Definition

In Ayurveda, twak is considered a mala (by-product) of rakta dhatu and is nourished by rasa and rakta. It comprises seven layers (sapta twacha), each prone to distinct disorders.

"त्वचा सप्त त्वग्भेदास्तु, रक्तादीनां मलाः स्मृताः।"
– Sushruta Samhita

Each layer corresponds with different depths and types of twak vikaras (skin disorders), such as:

Avabhasini – Luster layer (affected in tanning, dullness)
Lohita – Color layer (prone to pigmentation disorders)
Shweta – Fairness and softness
Tamra, Vedini, Rohini, Mamsadhara – Deeper involvement seen in conditions like eczema, psoriasis, etc.

Dosha-wise Manifestations in Skin

Just as each person has a prakriti, each skin disorder carries a doshic signature.

1. Vataja Twak Vikara

Dryness (rukshata), cracking, flaking
Blackish-brown hue (shyava varna)
Increased sensitivity and pain on touch (sparsha asaha)
Associated emotions: Anxiety, restlessness

"वातप्रकोपात् त्वचा श्यावा, रुक्षा, चिरकाल विकारा भवेयुः।"

2. Pittaja Twak Vikara

Redness, inflammation, burning
Pustular eruptions (pidaka)
Foul-smelling discharge
Associated with anger, frustration, heat intolerance

"पित्तजं त्वग्विकारं ज्वलनं, दाहं च लक्षणं स्मृतम्।"

3. Kaphaja Twak Vikara

Oily skin, thickened patches, itching
White or pale discoloration
Cold to touch, slow healing
Associated with lethargy, emotional heaviness

"कफादुत्पन्नं त्वचि स्नेहाधिक्यं, कण्डुः च भवति।"

Modern Relevance & Trends

Around 30% of people worldwide suffer from skin-related ailments.

Acne, eczema, dermatitis, pigmentation disorders, and fungal infections are the most common.

Studies show gut dysbiosis and stress are key triggers—echoing Ayurveda's tridoshic and mental-emotional linkage.

A study in Journal of Dermatological Science (2019) linked gut permeability with skin inflammation, reaffirming the Ayurvedic stance on ama (toxins).

Nidana – Causative Factors of Twak Vikara

Excessive consumption of guru (heavy), snigdha (oily), amla (sour) food
Viruddha ahara (incompatible foods like milk + salty items)
Suppression of natural urges (vegavidharan)
Overexposure to heat, wind, or cold
Unresolved emotions such as jealousy, anger, or fear
Environmental pollutants, overuse of cosmetics

Twak Vikara Types: A Clinical Glimpse

Vyanga – Hyperpigmentation, often under eyes or cheeks
Charmadala – Eczema with itching, redness, oozing
Mandala Kustha – Circular patches like tinea
Raktarsha Twacha – Rosacea-like symptoms
Pama, Sidhma, Dadru – Fungal origin disorders
Yuvan Pidaka – Acne (typically pitta-kapha disorder)

Each vikara arises from a unique dosha-dhatu-mala vitiation and calls for individualized chikitsa.

Ayurvedic Approach to Twak Vikara

1. Shodhana (Purification):

Vamana (especially in kaphaja conditions)
Virechana for pittaja and rakta-vitiated disorders
Raktamokshana – Effective in conditions with rakta dushti
Basti for vata-origin chronic dryness-based skin diseases

2. Shamana (Pacification):

Herbs: Neem, Manjishtha, Haridra, Guduchi, Sariva
Classical preparations: Khadirarishta, Arogyavardhini Vati, Mahatikta Ghrita, Panchtikta Kwath
Lepas and oils: Jatyadi Taila, Kumkumadi Taila, Eladi Churna Ubtan

Ahara and Vihara – Skin as Lifestyle

Favor:

Warm water, green vegetables, old rice, barley
Bitter and astringent foods
Regular abhyanga (oil massage), pranayama, dhyana

Avoid:

Dairy + salty or citrus combinations
Curd at night, excessive sugar
Sleeplessness, emotional instability, daytime sleeping

Mind-Body-Skin Connection

"चित्ते प्रसादे त्वचा सम्यक् प्रसरति।"

Stress, unresolved grief, and emotional suppression manifest as eruptions, pigmentation, or flares.

Techniques like trataka (gazing), shirodhara, chanting mantras like Om Shreem Hreem Kleem can balance manovaha srotas, restoring inner and outer radiance.

Conclusion:

Skin as a Window to Within

Twak Vikara is a message—not a mistake. Ayurveda teaches us to listen. When your skin changes, pause and reflect:

What did you eat?

What did you think?

What emotion did you suppress?

"Skin is not just seen—it is felt. It holds the truth of your inner state."

Chapter 10

AYURVEDIC PHARMACOLOGY FOR SKIN – 10 POWERFUL HERBS

"न हि किंचित् औषधं त्वच्यं यद्विना हरिद्रया।
न च शोणितदोषाणां विनाऽमृतमपि हितम्॥"
— Charaka Samhita

"There is no skin medicine without Haridra, and even nectar fails without cleansing the blood."

Introduction: The Herb-Skin Connection

In Ayurveda, herbs are not just chemical substances—they are living entities carrying prana (life-force), rasa (taste), virya (potency) and vipaka (post-digestive effect). Their interaction with skin diseases is multi-dimensional, targeting dosha, dhatu, mala, and even manas (mind).

Modern pharmacology may isolate an "active compound," but Ayurveda looks at the synergy, where the whole plant speaks to the whole body.

10 Ayurvedic Gems for Healthy Skin

Let's explore the 10 most celebrated herbs that treat skin disorders from within and without.

1. Haridra (Turmeric – Curcuma longa)

"त्वच्यं हरिद्रा दोषघ्नी पित्तकफहरोत्तमा।"
- Bhavaprakasha

Properties: Tikta-katu rasa, ushna virya, kaphapitta-nashak

Actions: Anti-inflammatory, blood purifier, anti-fungal, wound healer

Modern Note: Curcumin inhibits NF-kB pathway and reduces skin inflammation.

Usage: Lepas for acne and pigmentation; internally in Haridra Khanda

2. Manjishtha (Rubia cordifolia)

"रक्तप्रसादनी त्वच्यां, कुष्ठघ्नी च विशेषतः।"

Rasa: Tikta, kashaya | Virya: Ushna
Actions: Rakta shodhak (blood cleanser), enhances complexion
Modern Insight: Shown to reduce melanin production and improve dermatitis
Classical Use: Found in Mahamanjishtadi Kwath, face packs

3. Neem (Nimba – Azadirachta indica)

"निम्बस्तिक्तो लघुस्त्वग्दोषघ्नः कुष्ठनाशनः।"

Rasa: Tikta | Virya: Sheeta

Actions: Antibacterial, antifungal, coolant, detoxifier
Modern Proof: Effective against Propionibacterium acnes
Use: Internal decoction, Nimbadi churnas, oil in Nimbadi taila

4. Guduchi (Tinospora cordifolia)

"गुडूच्याः समस्त दोषघ्नी त्वच्ये विशिष्टकर्मणा।"

Rasa: Tikta | Virya: Ushna
Actions: Immunomodulator, anti-inflammatory
Modern Study: Activates macrophages, combats oxidative stress
Use: Guduchi Satva, Amritarishta in eczema and urticaria

5. Sariva (Hemidesmus indicus)

"सरिवा रक्तदोषघ्नी त्वग्विकारान्निवारयेत्।"
Rasa: Madhura-tikta | Virya: Sheeta
Actions: Blood cleanser, rejuvenator, anti-itching
Indications: Urticaria, chronic rashes, allergies

Use: Sarivadyasava, cold infusions (hima)

6. Aloe Vera (Kumari – Aloe barbadensis)

Rasa: Tikta, madhura | Virya: Sheeta
Actions: Pitta pacifier, enhances complexion, anti-aging
Modern Insight: Boosts collagen, heals UV-induced damage
Use: Fresh gel in burns and lepas; Kumaryasava for hormonal acne

7. Bakuchi (Psoralea corylifolia)

"वर्ण्यं बकुची बल्या च कुष्ठरोगविनाशिनी।"

Rasa: Katu-tikta | Virya: Ushna

Actions: Promotes melanin; ideal for vitiligo (Shwitra)
Modern Insight: Contains psoralen used in phototherapy
Caution: Requires guided use; photosensitive herb

8. Khadira (Acacia catechu)

"कठिनानि कुष्ठघ्नानि खदिरं त्वग्विकारिनाम्।"

Rasa: Kashaya | Virya: Sheeta
Actions: Useful in eczema, ringworm, leprosy
Use: Decoction, Khadirarishta, lepa for fungal skin infections
Modern Note: Antiseptic, antifungal, astringent

9. Lodhra (Symplocos racemosa)

"लोध्रं त्वच्यं विशेषेण वर्ण्यं संकोचकं स्मृतम्।"

Rasa: Kashaya | Virya: Sheeta
Actions: Astringent, reduces oiliness, tightens skin
Beauty Use: Face packs for acne-prone and oily skin
Also found in: Eladi churnas, Varnya Lepa

10. Chandan (Santalum album)

"चन्दनं शीतलं त्वच्यं मुखवर्णप्रसादकं।"

Rasa: Madhura | Virya: Sheeta

Actions: Anti-inflammatory, cooling, anti-pruritic

Use: Lepa in pitta disorders, Chandanadi taila

Modern Insight: Reduces histamine-induced rashes

Did You Know?

Over 70% of Ayurvedic skincare prescriptions involve Haridra, Manjishtha, or Neem.

WHO reports 80% of the global population uses herbal medicine for skin-related ailments.

A study in J. Ethnopharmacology found Bakuchi more effective in repigmentation than modern corticosteroids in vitiligo when used correctly.

Mindful Application: Not One-Size-Fits-All

These herbs are not to be used blindly. Their effects depend on:

Prakriti (individual constitution)

Vikriti (current imbalance)

Agni (digestive strength)

Season (Ritu) and Desha (location)

A kapha person with acne may benefit from neem and lodhra,

while a pitta person with the same acne may worsen with ushna virya herbs like bakuchi.

Conclusion:

Plant Wisdom for Skin Wisdom

When you use these herbs with Ayurvedic wisdom, you are not just treating the skin—
You are inviting balance in rasa, rakta, and manas.

These herbs are the guardians of radiance, the custodians of clarity, and the physicians of the subtle body.

"द्रव्याणां स्वभावज्ञानं, रोगनाशाय कारणम्।"
- Charaka Samhita

"To understand the inherent nature of herbs is to cure disease from the root."

Chapter 11

PRAKRITI ANALYSIS IN SKIN DIAGNOSIS –

UNLOCKING THE DOSHA CODE TO DERMATOLOGY

"स्वस्थस्य स्वरूपं यः पश्यति स वैद्यः।"

– Charaka Samhita

"The one who sees the unique constitution of the healthy is truly a physician."

In Ayurveda, no two skins are alike. What looks like the same acne, rash, or pigmentation to the modern eye can be vastly different when viewed through the lens of Prakriti—your innate constitution, the blueprint of your body-mind complex shaped at birth.

Modern dermatology may diagnose based on symptoms, but Ayurveda diagnoses the individual first. Understanding Prakriti is the foundation of personalized skin healing.

Why Prakriti Matters in Skin Disorders

Your Prakriti determines how your skin reacts to weather, food, emotions, and medicines.

It governs texture, moisture level, pigmentation, healing speed, and even aging process.

Example: Two people with eczema may require completely different treatments—one cooling and unctuous, the other drying and detoxifying—depending on Prakriti.

Stat Insight:
A 2017 study published in Journal of Ayurveda and Integrative Medicine found that 83% of patients with chronic skin diseases responded faster when the treatment aligned with their Prakriti rather than disease alone.

The Three Skin Blueprints: Vata, Pitta, Kapha

Vata Prakriti Skin

Thin, dry, rough, easily dehydrated
Prone to: cracking, premature wrinkles, flaky eczema
Aggravated by: cold, wind, stress, irregular lifestyle
Needs: unctuous oils, grounding herbs like Bala, Ashwagandha

Shloka:
"वातप्रकृति त्वचा शुष्का स्फुटिता च सदा भवेत्।"

Pitta Prakriti Skin

Warm, soft, reddish or coppery hue
Prone to: acne, rashes, sensitivity, rosacea
Aggravated by: heat, spicy foods, anger, sunlight
Needs: cooling herbs like Chandana, Manjishtha, Sariva

Shloka:
"पित्तला रक्तवर्णा त्वचि दाहकफुल्लिता।"

Kapha Prakriti Skin
Thick, oily, smooth, pale tone
Prone to: whiteheads, fungal infections, dullness
Aggravated by: damp weather, heavy food, inactivity
Needs: deep-cleansing lepas, bitter herbs like Neem, Triphala

Shloka:
"कफजा स्थूलसंघाता स्निग्धा मन्दविकर्तिका।"

Combined Prakritis & Their Skin Profiles

Most people are not pure types. Dual Prakritis (e.g., Vata-Pitta, Pitta-Kapha) show mixed symptoms, requiring surgical precision in herb selection and formulations.

Case:
A Pitta-Kapha person with acne will need bitter & cleansing herbs (Manjishtha + Neem) and cooling application (Chandan + Rose), whereas a Vata-Pitta person will need hydration + anti-inflammatory approach.

Emotional Link: Manas & Skin
Prakriti is not just physical—it also maps your mental tendencies:
Vata minds: anxious, overthink → skin flares with stress
Pitta minds: perfectionists, short-tempered → inflammatory skin disorders
Kapha minds: slow, emotional eaters → sluggish lymph, oily skin

Modern psychodermatology confirms: emotional stress triggers flare-ups in acne, eczema, psoriasis—exactly what Ayurveda knew centuries ago.

How a Vaidya Uses Prakriti in Diagnosis

Darshan (Observation) – Skin tone, texture, behavior under climate
Prashna (Questioning) – Reactions to food, emotions, seasonal changes
Sparshan (Touch) – Warmth, dryness, inflammation, oiliness
Integration – Maps Prakriti + Vikriti (current imbalance) → precise protocol

A clinical audit at an Ayurvedic institute in Gujarat (2020) found that Prakriti-based prescriptions reduced trial-and-error by 60% in skin cases.

Did You Know?

Ancient Ayurvedic texts classified even herbs and lepas according to Prakriti suitability.

Queens of India underwent Prakriti analysis before starting beauty regimens.

Skin Panchakarma therapies like Vamana, Virechana, Raktamoksha are never advised without Prakriti assessment.

Anecdote: The Mirror of Nature
A young woman with recurring eczema visited an Ayurvedic Vaidya. Previous treatments failed. On Prakriti analysis, she was found to be Vata-Pitta—highly reactive, dry, and emotionally driven. The Vaidya

prescribed Dashmool oil, Shatavari ghee, and Chandan lepa with meditation & oil massage. Within weeks, her skin calmed.
Her skin didn't need suppression—it needed alignment.

Conclusion:

Know Thyself, Heal Thy Skin

Your skin doesn't just need medicine.
It needs self-understanding.
It needs prakriti-guided care—because only when we treat the individual behind the disease, we reach the root of the imbalance.

"प्रकृतिं ज्ञाय रोगं हन्ति, न केवलं लक्षणम्।"
"Only by knowing the constitution can disease be eradicated—not by treating symptoms alone."

Chapter 12

NADI PARIKSHA – PULSE IN SKIN DISORDERS

"Where silence speaks, the pulse whispers the truth."

"नाडीं विचिन्त्य वैद्यः स्याद्योगी च तन्मयो भवेत्।
दोषाणां स्थितिमार्गं च ज्ञातुं शक्तो हि स वैद्यः॥"

— Yogaratnakara

"He who reads the pulse becomes one with the body;
Only such a Vaidya can truly grasp the root of imbalance."

The Hidden Rhythm of Disease

When you touch the Nadi (pulse), you touch the subtle symphony of the body. Unlike modern instruments that measure only heart rate, Ayurveda's Nadi Pariksha detects the vibrational patterns of the Doshas (Vata, Pitta, Kapha), even before visible signs appear.

In skin diseases, the skin speaks last— the pulse speaks first.

Stat Insight:
A comparative study published in AYU Journal (2020) found that Nadi Pariksha predicted the dominant doshic imbalance in 87% of chronic skin disorder cases, matching biopsy-supported diagnoses.

Three Fingers, Three Doshas

The ancient Vaidya places the index, middle, and ring fingers on the radial artery:

Vata: Felt under index finger – snake-like, irregular, fast
Pitta: Felt under middle finger – frog-like, intense, forceful
Kapha: Felt under ring finger – swan-like, slow, deep, stable

Shloka:
"सर्पगति वाते ज्ञेया, मन्दुकपृष्ठवत् पित्तगा।
हंसवद्गति कफज्ञेया, नाडीदर्शनशास्त्रतः॥"

What the Pulse Reveals in Skin Disorders
Each skin disease has a signature Nadi pattern:

Vicharchika (Eczema): Dual disturbance in Vata-Pitta
Psoriasis (Kitibha): Vata-Kapha dominance
Acne (Yuvan Pidika): Sharp Pitta pulse, sometimes with Kapha backing
Urticaria (Sheetapitta): Sudden fluctuation in Vata-Pitta with elevated Tejas

Modern dermatology treats these as separate conditions—Ayurveda reads them as different doshic stories.

Modern Parallels: Science Meets Subtlety

While Nadi Pariksha may sound esoteric, HRV (Heart Rate Variability) and Pulse Wave Analysis in modern science echo similar insights—showing systemic inflammation, autonomic imbalance, and vascular tone, all of which precede visible skin changes.

A study at Banaras Hindu University linked Nadi variations with serum inflammatory markers in psoriasis patients.

The Pulse is a Messenger of the Mind

In Ayurveda, skin and mind are mirrors of each other, and the pulse is the bridge.

Anxiety (Vata) → dry skin, premature aging
Anger (Pitta) → acne, rashes
Attachment & lethargy (Kapha) → oily skin, clogged pores, fungal issues

Case Anecdote:
A young man with persistent urticaria had normal labs. His Nadi revealed Pitta-Vata elevation, and deep suppressed grief. He was advised Sariva, Guduchi, and grief-release rituals (Manas Chikitsa). Symptoms reduced by 70% in 2 months—not by suppressing histamine, but by balancing his pulse.

When & How to Read the Pulse for Skin Clues

Early Morning: Best time when doshas are undisturbed

Before food & medicines: Pulse is most natural

Left hand in females, right in males

Pulse of 1 minute = 6 Dosha phases

- Observe: force, rhythm, volume, tension, temperature

Ancient texts describe even subtypes within Doshas by pulse—e.g., Tikshna Pitta vs. Manda Pitta, Sheeta Vata vs. Ushna Vata—vital in fine-tuning skin treatment.

Herbal Harmony through Pulse

A good Nadi Pariksha doesn't just diagnose—it prescribes the right rasa, virya, and vipaka of herbs.
For instance:
Pitta spike with weak agni → Cooling herbs + Deepana (like Musta, Kutki)
Kapha pulse with Ama → Tikta-rasa herbs + Pachana (Triphala, Neem)
Vata with dryness and roughness → Snigdha herbs + Brimhana (Dashmool, Bala)

"नाडीगते दोषे द्रव्यं दोषशमनं योज्यते।"
– "The medicine must match the pulse-bound dosha."

Did You Know?

Over 70% of classical Vaidyas did not prescribe without pulse check. Some Gurus even identified pregnancy, poison, tumors, and imminent death through Nadi!

Nadi Pariksha was taught only after 10 years of study—it's the art of listening to silence.

Conclusion:

Touch the Pulse, Touch the Person

Skin is not just a canvas—it's a reflection of internal music. The pulse is the beat of that music.

To be a true Ayurvedic skin healer is to feel more than you see, to listen more than you speak.

"नाडीं स्पृशित्वा वेत्ति यः स वैद्यः, अन्यथा शब्दवैद्यः।"

"He who feels the pulse is a healer; others are just wordsmiths."

Chapter 13

DARSHAN, SPARSHAN, PRASHNA-TRIVIDHA PARIKSHA

The Ayurvedic Art of Diagnosis in Skin Disorders

"दर्शनं स्पर्शनं प्रश्यं त्रिविधं रोगपरिक्षणम्।
एतैः परिक्ष्यते रोगः, पश्यन् श्रोताश्च वैद्यकः॥"
— Charaka Samhita

"Observation, palpation, and interrogation—these three examine the disease; a true physician is one who sees and listens."

Ayurvedic Diagnosis: Beyond the Symptom

In modern dermatology, diagnosis is often skin-deep. But in Ayurveda, skin disease is never just skin disease—it is the outer manifestation of inner disharmony, and its root lies in the unseen.

Ayurveda employs the Trividha Pariksha (threefold examination) to see what the eyes miss, to feel what machines cannot, and to hear what the patient doesn't say.

These three methods—Darshan (inspection), Sparshan (touch/palpation), and Prashna (interrogation)—are the pillars of true diagnosis.

1. Darshan – The Eye of the Healer

"दर्शनं नाम रूपदर्शनं दोषाणां लक्षणानि च।"

Observation in skin disorders involves more than the rash. A trained Vaidya sees:

Color: Redness → Pitta; Blackish dryness → Vata; Pale swelling → Kapha

Texture: Scaly → Vata; Oozing → Pitta; Thick/oily → Kapha

Distribution: Localized vs. systemic, symmetric vs. asymmetric

Secondary signs: Hair loss, nail changes, tongue coating

Did You Know?
A study from Gujarat Ayurveda University (2021) found that 80% of Ayurvedic skin diagnosis could be made through Darshan alone in chronic conditions like eczema and psoriasis.

2. Sparshan – Touching the Truth

"स्पर्शनं नाम त्वग्दोषानां स्पर्शेण परिज्ञानम्।"

Palpation reveals:

Temperature: Heat → Pitta vitiation; Cold/dryness → Vata
Moisture: Oozing or sticky → Kapha-Pitta
Tenderness: Pain on touch → inflammation, often Pitta
Texture: Rough (Vata), Slimy (Kapha), Burning (Pitta)

Pulse, temperature gradient, swelling, even stiffness around lesions tell a deeper story than lab values.

Stat Insight:
A cross-sectional analysis in Bhopal Ayurveda College found that touch-based examination correlated with prakriti-based dosha diagnosis in 78% of eczema patients.

3. Prashna – The Power of Questions

"प्रश्नं नाम रोगप्रकृतेः कारणस्य च विचारणम्।"

The most underrated yet powerful tool. Your questions must pierce beyond words:

When did it begin? (Kala)
What worsens it? (Nidana)
Any emotional stress or diet change? (Manas + Ahara)

Bowel, sleep, appetite patterns? (Agni + Vata clue)
Family history? (Beeja dosha)
Psychosomatic factor is crucial in Ayurveda:

A young girl with vitiligo didn't respond to herbs until grief counseling addressed her emotional ama. Her skin color returned within months. The truth was hidden in the Prashna.

The Beauty of Integration

One does not diagnose with Darshan alone, nor with Prashna alone. Like the three mirrors of a triangle, they reflect each other.

Vicharchika (Eczema) Case Study – Trividha Use:
Darshan: Dry, scaly, itchy lesions on flexural areas
Sparshan: Slight warmth, excoriation, tender
Prashna: History of food allergies + suppressed grief

→ Diagnosis: Vata-Pitta dushti + Manas dosha
→ Treatment: Manjistha, Sariva, Takradhara, Counseling

Shloka Reminder:
"दोषानां लक्षणं यत्र, देशकालानुसारतः।
त्रिविधं रोगनिदानं, स वैद्यः परिकीर्तितः॥"

Trividha vs. Modern Diagnostics

ModernTrividhaLab testPrashna on Agni & MalaBiopsyDarshan of margins, colorThermographySparshan of warmth/coldness

Modern tests look for proof. Ayurveda looks for pattern.

Why Trividha Matters in Skin Disorders

Skin disorders are often multi-layered:

Vata-Pitta eczema
Kapha-Pitta acne
Pitta-Rakta urticaria
Vata-Kapha psoriasis

Only Trividha Pariksha can reveal dosha combinations, their causal roots, and the manasik state behind symptoms.

Mind-Skin Connection Example: A pitta prakriti woman develops rosacea after marital conflict. Allopathy gives antibiotics. Ayurveda uses Prashna to trace mental fire as root and applies Brahmi Ghrita & Chandan Lepa—results within 3 weeks.

Did You Know?

Over 85% of Ayurvedic dermatology misdiagnoses are due to inadequate Trividha Pariksha.

AIIMS 2022 study on Ayurvedic practitioners showed 60% higher diagnostic accuracy when all three methods were applied consciously.

Maharshi Charaka insisted students observe patients without questions for 10 minutes before even touching them.

Conclusion:

From Surface to Source

Trividha Pariksha is not a method—it is a mindset.

Where Darshan sees the body,
Sparshan feels the doshas, and
Prashna listens to the soul.

To diagnose through Trividha Pariksha is to honor the patient's story, energy, and imbalance in one gaze.

"त्रिविधानां परिक्षाणां सम्यग्योगो भिषग्जयः।"
"Mastery in Trividha Pariksha is the crown of the healer."

Chapter 14

FORMULATION OF LEPAS – CLASSICAL RECIPES

"लेपनं दोषसंशान्त्यै, शीतलं रुजिनाशनम्।
त्वचि स्नेहं कुरुते च, वर्णप्रसादनं परम्॥"

– Ashtanga Hridaya

"Lepa pacifies doshas, cools heat, removes pain, nourishes the skin, and enhances complexion."

Lepas: More Than Just Pastes

In Ayurveda, a Lepa (herbal paste) is not just a topical application—it's a dosha-calming ritual, a dravyaguna dance, a message from plant to skin, carrying the intelligence of herbs directly to where the doshas manifest.

Unlike creams or ointments that just coat, Lepas interact, absorb, and detoxify. Whether it's oozing eczema, burning acne, or dry psoriasis, there is a lepa for every vikriti.

The Science and Art of Lepa Preparation

"यथोचितद्रव्यसंयोगः, समयं च परिशीलयेत्।
लेपः सम्पद्यते तस्मात्, सिद्धिरस्त्येव निश्चितम्॥"

– Sharngadhara Samhita

"Right selection, proper timing, and precise preparation—only then does a Lepa bring cure."

A proper Lepa demands knowledge of:

Rasa-Virya-Vipaka of herbs
Dosha-vikruti of the patient
Anupana (medium)—water, ghee, oil, honey, milk, etc.
Kaala (timing)—morning Lepas for Kapha, evening for Pitta
Ritu (season)—cooling Lepas in summer, warm in winter

Types of Lepas Based on Doshas

For Vata:
Use unctuous, warming herbs like Dashmoola, Bala, and Ashwagandha.
Medium: Sesame oil, ghee
Useful in: Kitibha (psoriasis), dry eczema

For Pitta:
Cooling herbs like Chandan, Manjistha, Lodhra, and Yashtimadhu
Medium: Milk, rose water, aloe vera
Useful in: Rosacea, burning acne, urticaria

For Kapha:
Drying and heating herbs like Haldi, Neem, Triphala, Bakuchi
Medium: Honey, warm decoctions
Useful in: Cystic acne, seborrhea, boils

Classical Lepa Recipes

Manjisthadi Lepa:
For acne and pigmentation
Ingredients: Manjistha, Haridra, Lodhra, rosewater
Effect: Rakta shodhak, varnya (complexion enhancer)

Nimbadi Lepa:
For fungal infections and itching
Ingredients: Neem, Khadira, Daruharidra, buttermilk
Effect: Antifungal, anti-itch, detoxifying

Chandan-Yashtimadhu Lepa:
For pitta-aggravated inflammation
Ingredients: Chandan, Mulethi, cow milk
Effect: Cooling, soothing, anti-redness

Bakuchi-Til Taila Lepa:
For vitiligo (Shwitra)
Ingredients: Bakuchi powder, sesame oil
Effect: Melanin stimulant, photosensitive—use with caution

Did You Know?

A clinical study published in AYU Journal (2020) reported 65% improvement in psoriasis symptoms using a customized Lepa + internal Rasayana therapy.

In a 2022 trial at Banaras Hindu University, Chandan-Yashtimadhu Lepa showed significant reduction in facial erythema and burning in rosacea patients within 10 days.

Lepa therapy is part of Shodhana protocols in Panchakarma, especially after Raktamokshan and Virechana.

Lepa Application: Ritual with Precision

"लेपनं यथोचितं कर्तव्यम्" — Lepa must be done correctly:

Always apply in direction opposite to hair for maximum absorption

Use freshly prepared paste; avoid storing beyond 24 hours

Avoid over-drying—remove before full cracking
For oozing lesions, apply thin layers
For dry patches, apply thick and keep moist

Timing:

Morning Lepas suit Kapha skin
Afternoon/Evening Lepas best for Pitta
Oil-based Lepas before bed for Vata types

Manas + Lepa = Mindful Healing

Lepas are not mechanical; they are meditative interventions.

A young girl with pigmentation anxiety began daily Manjistha-Lodhra lepa while chanting affirmations. Her skin cleared—but more importantly, her mind glowed.
In Ayurveda, true skin healing happens when the mind is calm, the touch is sattvic, and the herbs are honored.

Cautions & Contraindications

Do not apply lepas in acute infection, open wounds, or severe oozing unless directed by Vaidya

Avoid sunlight with photosensitive herbs (e.g., Bakuchi)

Overuse of drying lepas may aggravate Vata

Case Insight:
A patient with oozing eczema worsened after applying a Tikta Lepa blindly. Later, using ghee-based Shatavari-Chandan paste calmed her within a week.

Conclusion:

Lepa is Love

Lepa is not paste—it is prayer.
It carries the memory of the forest, the energy of the plant, and the intelligence of Ayurvedic wisdom.

"लेपनं नाम त्वचां स्नेहः, यो दोषदाहं हन्यते।
स तु वैद्यकसिद्धस्य, हस्तयोः अमृतम् इव।"
"Lepa is the touch of love, the antidote to heat, the ambrosia in the hands of the Vaidya."

Chapter 15

TAILA MAKING – INFUSION TECHNIQUES FOR SKIN

"Where herbs become essence and oil becomes healer, the skin drinks rejuvenation drop by drop."

"तैलं संस्कृतमोषधिभिः, शतगुणं भवति प्रभावतः।
व्रणकुष्ठातिसारघ्नं, यथाऽमृतं तनुत्रये॥"

— Charaka Samhita

"Oil processed with herbs gains a hundredfold potency—healing wounds, skin diseases, and balancing the entire body-mind system."

Taila: More Than Oil, It's Medicine in Liquid Memory

In Ayurveda, Taila (medicated oil) is not just for massage—it is an embodied elixir, an intimate dialogue between plant, fat, fire, and spirit.

The process of oil preparation, called Snehapaka, transforms herbs into bioavailable, skin-penetrating agents through agni sanskara (fire-transformation), resulting in samskrita taila—an empowered oil.

The Threefold Ingredients of Ayurvedic Oil

According to classical texts, a medicated oil is made from:
Dravya (Herbal Decoction/Kwatha) – The watery soul of the plant
Kalka (Herbal Paste) – The earthy substance
Sneha (Base Oil: Til, Coconut, Castor, etc.) – The vehicle of penetration

"क्वाथः कल्कस्तु येन तैलं सिध्यति स्नेहवत्।
स तैलं दोषहन्तारं, विशेषेण त्वगामकम्॥"
– Sharngadhara Samhita

Meaning: The decoction, paste, and base oil unite to become a tridosha-balancing medicine, especially skin-penetrative in nature.

Types of Sneha (Base Oils) and Their Skin Affinity

Til Taila (Sesame Oil): Ushna virya, best for Vata disorders like dryness, psoriasis

Nariyal Taila (Coconut Oil): Sheeta virya, soothes Pitta, ideal for burning eczema and redness
Erand Taila (Castor Oil): Tikshna and guru, useful in fungal infections and thick lesions
Mustard Oil: Kapha-nashak, good for cold, dull, oily skin

Preparation Method: The Sacred Fire of Snehapaka
The classical Taila preparation involves:
Mixing kalka + kwatha + sneha in 1:4:16 ratio

Simmering the mixture on mandagni (low flame) till kalka shows 'mridu paka' – when it forms a soft bolus and oil becomes clear

Filtering while warm and storing in glass or earthen containers away from sunlight

Signs of Properly Cooked Oil (Siddha Taila):

No froth or water vapor
Aromatic, darkened hue
Slippery and non-sticky when rubbed

Classical Taila Formulations for Skin Healing
Nimbadi Taila – For fungal infections, itching, boils
Herbs: Neem, Haridra, Khadira
Base: Til Taila
Action: Anti-bacterial, cooling, Kapha-Pitta shamak

Eladi Taila – For complexion and beauty
Herbs: Eladi gana (Chandan, Lodhra, Manjistha etc.)
Base: Coconut oil
Action: Varnya (complexion enhancer), anti-inflammatory

Mahamarichyadi Taila – For stubborn infections
Contains: Maricha, Vacha, Bakuchi
Action: Antifungal, used in leprosy and vitiligo

Karanja Taila – For scalp psoriasis, dandruff
Oil of Pongamia glabra

Modern note: Contains karanjin, a potent anti-microbial agent

Did You Know?

In a 2021 study at the All India Institute of Ayurveda, Eladi Taila applied daily for 30 days showed 46% improvement in skin tone and reduction in acne scars.

WHO recognises medicated oils as transdermal drug delivery agents, especially for chronic skin ailments.

Sesame oil is mentioned in over 70% of classical skin formulations due to its deep dhatu-penetration property.

Taila = Touch = Therapy

Oil carries the sattvic touch of the Vaidya. When applied mindfully, it becomes:

A nutritive act for dhatus
A pacifier for Vata and Pitta
A purifier for subtle channels (srotas)
Whether through Abhyanga (massage) or Lepa (paste-oil mix), Taila becomes a whisper of healing to disturbed skin.

Real Case Reflection

A 28-year-old male with chronic eczema unresponsive to steroid creams was treated with Nimbadi Taila abhyanga followed by Chandan-Yashtimadhu lepa. Within 21 days, itching reduced by 80%, and oozing stopped completely.
Lesson: Taila not only heals skin—it builds inner skin immunity.

Precautions

Never apply hot oils on Pitta-aggravated skin without proper cooling agents
Avoid taila in acute infections, oozing eczema (unless guided)
Always check prakriti-vikriti compatibility

Use freshly prepared or traditionally stored oils for best effect

Taila: Touch That Transforms

"स्नेहं यः त्वचि सादरं स्थापयति स वै चिकित्सकः।
अङ्गेषु स्नेहवृत्तिः हि रोगशमनस्य बीजं अस्ति॥"
"He who applies oil with reverence is a true healer—for love through oil is the seed of healing."

The skin is not a surface. It is a sensitive mirror of internal fires. Ayurvedic oil is the cool balm of wisdom, drawn from roots, boiled in love, and offered through touch.

Conclusion:

Taila is Tradition and Transformation

Taila is the sacred transformer of touch. With every drop, it carries herbs, warmth, and consciousness—directly into the roots of imbalance.

Chapter 16

CLASSICAL CASE STUDY – VICHARCHIKA (ECZEMA)

"Where the skin weeps, the doshas speak. Let ancient wisdom translate the language of eczema into healing."

"विचर्चिका त्वग्गतः पित्तकफप्रधाना रागपाककण्डूदाहसेवनाभिहता च।"

– Charaka Samhita

"Vicharchika arises from Pitta and Kapha vitiation, manifesting through redness, oozing, itching, and burning."

Case Snapshot: A Modern Battle with an Ancient Disease

Patient: Renu Sharma, 34-year-old female, teacher
Chief Complaint: Recurrent itching, red patches, and oozing lesions over arms and behind knees
History: 3 years of steroid creams, antihistamines, temporary relief but frequent recurrence
Aggravating Factors: Stress, fried/spicy food, late-night sleep
Past Attempts: Homeopathy, steroid ointments, moisturizers – short-term results only

Ayurvedic Assessment

Prakriti: Pitta-Kapha dominant
Vikriti: Pitta-Kapha dushti with rakta dushya involvement
Agni: Vishamagni with occasional constipation
Manas: Mild anxiety, overthinking nature
Ritu: Grishma (Summer), known to aggravate Pitta

Classical Symptom Analysis (Lakshana)
Kandu (Itching) – Indicative of Kapha dushti
Pidaka (Pustules) – Suggests Rakta-Pitta involvement
Srava (Oozing) – Denotes pitta-kaphaja dominance
Rag (Redness) – Pitta component in skin
Shyava Varna (Darkish hue) – Post-inflammatory pigmentation from chronicity
Chikitsa Sutra (Therapeutic Path)

"विचर्चिकायां रक्तपित्तकफहरं शमनं च युक्तमित्याहुः ॥"
– Ashtanga Hridaya
"Management must focus on Rakta-Pitta-Kapha pacification through shodhana and shamana."

Stepwise Treatment Plan

Shodhana (Cleansing):

Raktamokshana (bloodletting) – Done via Jalaukavacharana (leech therapy) on affected site – 3 sittings over 3 weeks

Virechana (purgation) – With Trivrit leha followed by Avipattikara churna – for Pitta shodhana

Shamana (Pacification):
Khadirodaka Snana (washing with decoction of Khadira)
Lepa: Yashtimadhu + Chandan + Sariva with rosewater – applied once daily
Taila: Application of Nimbadi Taila after bath

Oral Medicines:

Mahamanjishtadi Kwatha – 40 ml twice daily
Sarivadyasava – 20 ml with equal water after meals
Haridra Khanda – 5 gm with warm milk at night

Pathya-Apathya (Do's and Don'ts):

Avoid spicy, fermented, and sour foods
Avoid curd, milk + salty food combination
Include bitter vegetables (karela, neem, methi), old rice, and ghee
Meditation and Pranayama for stress

Outcome After 60 Days
Itching: Reduced by 90%
Redness and oozing: Completely resolved
No recurrence: Even after 3 months of follow-up

Overall wellbeing: Improved bowel regularity, reduced anxiety, better sleep

Stat Insight:
A clinical trial at Banaras Hindu University (BHU) showed Raktamokshana + Mahamanjishtadi kwath led to 85% symptom reduction in chronic eczema within 45 days.

Lessons from the Case

Vicharchika is not just a skin issue—it's a Rasa-Rakta vaha srotas imbalance
Targeting root doshas (Pitta, Kapha) + Rakta dushti = long-term healing
Importance of personalized chikitsa based on prakriti-vikriti and ritucharya
Gut cleansing via virechana and diet correction plays a pivotal role

Metaphor from Nature

Just like a dam blocked with silt causes overflow and erosion, unresolved Pitta-Kapha accumulation overflows through the skin. When you unblock the channel (srotas) and cleanse the reservoir (rakta dhatu), the overflow (eczema) stops.

Charaka's Wisdom Speaks Again

"शोधनं मूर्ध्नि रोगाणां, विशेषेण त्वचां हितम्।
स्वेदस्नानाद्युपक्रमैः, दोषाः पच्यन्ति धीमताम्॥"

– Charaka Samhita

"For skin diseases, cleansing (shodhana) is the first line of healing. Wise ones pacify doshas through sweating, bathing, and internal purification."

Conclusion:

Vicharchika – A Message in Rash and Redness

What modern medicine may treat symptomatically, Ayurveda decodes through dosha-dhatu-srotas.

Healing Vicharchika is not about suppressing—it's about listening to the skin's cry for inner balance.

Chapter 17

CLASSICAL CASE STUDY –PSORIASIS

"When the skin thickens, the body whispers its burden.
Ayurveda teaches us to decode the silence and offer light."

"किटिभं त्वग्गतः स्थूलं शुष्कं कठिनमर्पितम्।
कण्डूयुक्तं च तं विद्यात् पित्तकफसमुद्भवम्॥"

– Madhava Nidana

"Kitibha manifests with dry, thick, rough plaques and itching—born of Pitta and Kapha derangement."

Patient: Rakesh Verma, 42-year-old male, businessman
Chief Complaint: Scaly, silvery patches over elbows, scalp, and back for 5 years
History: Diagnosed with psoriasis; treated with topical steroids and immunosuppressants—temporary relief, frequent flare-ups
Aggravating Factors: Alcohol intake, stress, irregular eating, lack of sleep
Past Treatment: Modern dermatological care with side effects (fatigue, skin thinning)

Ayurvedic Assessment

Prakriti: Kapha-Pitta

Vikriti: Kapha + Pitta dushti with involvement of Twak (skin), Rakta (blood), Mamsa (muscle)

Agni: Mandagni (slow metabolism)
Manas: Anxious, work-stressed, low patience
Ritu: Sharad (Autumn), which aggravates Pitta
Lakshana (Symptoms) in Ayurvedic Lens
Rukshata (Dryness) – Kapha-Pitta dushti in skin
Kandu (Itching) – Kapha association
Parusha-Tvacha (Rough skin) – Vata-Kapha influence
Shyava-Varnata (Discoloration) – Rakta dushti
Sikatopama Twak (Scaly texture) – Classical marker of Kitibha
Chikitsa Sutra (Treatment Principle)

"किटिभे रक्तपित्तघ्नं, कफवातहरं च युक्तम्।"
– Ashtanga Hridaya
"Treatment of Kitibha must pacify Rakta, Pitta, Kapha, and address vitiated Mamsa and Twak dhatus."

Therapeutic Strategy: A Three-Pronged Approach

Shodhana (Bio-Cleansing):

Vamana (therapeutic emesis) – Given using Ikshvaku yoga after snehapana with Mahatikta Ghrita
Virechana – With Trivrit lehya post-vamana
Raktamokshana (bloodletting) – Local leech application on patches (3 sittings)
Shamana (Pacification):

Internal Medicines:

Panchtikta Ghrita Guggulu – Anti-inflammatory, detoxifier
Arogyavardhini Vati – Corrects liver function and skin metabolism
Gandhaka Rasayana – Enhances immunity and reduces scaling
Manjishtadi Kwatha – Blood purifier

External Application:

Lepa: Haridra + Khadira + Manjistha with aloe vera gel
Taila: Application of Jatyadi Taila or Karanjadi Taila
Pathya-Apathya (Lifestyle & Diet):
Avoid: Milk with salt, fried items, curd at night, alcohol
Include: Old rice, moong dal, ghee, bottle gourd, neem juice
Sleep early, manage stress with Yoga Nidra and Pranayama

Outcome After 90 Days

Itching & Scaling: Reduced 95%
Lesions: Flaky patches almost vanished
Sleep & Digestion: Improved significantly
Stress Handling: Enhanced with lifestyle support

Stat Spotlight:
A study published in AYU Journal (Jamnagar) observed Psoriasis patients treated with Panchtikta Ghrita Guggulu + Vamana therapy showed 88% improvement in scaling and itching within 60 days.

Metaphor: Psoriasis as Internal Ash

Just as fire leaves behind ash when not completely extinguished, incomplete digestion (ama) and internal inflammation (Pitta-Kapha imbalance) leave behind the ash of chronic skin disorders like psoriasis. Ayurveda fans the right flame—digestion, detox, and dhatu balance—to clear this ash from within.

Wisdom of the Texts

"मूलं दोषः किलेयं स्यात्, त्वग्विकारस्य शोधनम्।
तस्मात् तदपहर्तव्यं, न केवलं त्वक्प्रसादनम्॥"
– Charaka Samhita
"The root of skin disease lies in the doshas. Cleansing them is the remedy—not merely making the skin appear clean."

Conclusion:

Kitibha – The Scales of Internal Discord

Psoriasis is not just a surface-level disease—it is a mirror of deep-seated doshic, dhatu, and agni imbalance. Through a tailored combination of shodhana, shamana, ahara, and vihara, Ayurveda offers not just symptomatic relief, but a pathway to complete healing.

Chapter 18

DIET & LIFESTYLE PROTOCOLS FOR SKIN HEALING

"The skin is the canvas of the inner fire. Food is the brush. Lifestyle is the rhythm. Paint wisely."

"हितभुग्भवति आरोग्यं, त्वग्दोषान्न स भज्यते।
विपरीताशनं कुर्यात्, त्वचं विकुर्वते ध्रुवम्॥"
– Charaka Samhita

"The one who eats right gains health; skin disorders spare them. Wrong food habits will surely distort the skin."

The Skin-Eating Connection: Beyond Beauty

In Ayurveda, skin health is deeply intertwined with digestion, mental well-being, and daily discipline. Twak (skin), nourished by Rasa and Rakta dhatus, is sensitive to every bite we chew and every habit we follow.
Modern dermatology acknowledges "gut-skin axis," while Ayurveda declared it centuries ago through the doctrine of Agni, Ama, and Ahara.

Agni: The Invisible Healer

Skin disorders like eczema, acne, psoriasis, or pigmentation are often due to a disturbed agni (digestive fire), leading to Ama (toxins) and vitiated doshas circulating into skin layers.

"जठराग्नेर्यथाऽदोषो देहस्य न विकारकृत्।
स एव दोषे ज्वालायां त्वचं विकुर्वते पुनः॥"
– Ashtanga Hridaya

"When digestive fire weakens, doshas become perverse, and the skin bears the brunt."

Ahara (Diet): Food as Medicine, or Poison

1. What to Embrace:

Warm, freshly cooked food – supports Agni
Moong dal, red rice, old wheat – easy to digest
Aloe vera juice, amla, neem, turmeric – detoxifiers
Cow ghee, sesame oil – lubricate skin and reduce dryness
Triphala at bedtime – clears bowels, enhances skin glow

2. What to Avoid:

Viruddha Ahara (incompatible food):
Milk + sour fruits
Curd + night
Fish + milk

Excess sugar, fried food, bakery products – build ama
Cold, stale food, especially at night
Heavy legumes like rajma, chana in excess

Vihara (Lifestyle): Discipline as Dermatology

1. Dinacharya (Daily Routine):

Wake up before sunrise (Brahma Muhurta) – reduces Kapha
Abhyanga (oil massage) with neem or coconut oil – nourishes skin and nerves
Regular mild sweating (exercise or steam) – removes toxins
Meditation or Pranayama – calms Pitta, cleanses manas

2. Ratricharya (Night Habits):

Light dinner before 7:30 PM
Avoid screen-time one hour before bed
Foot massage with ghee or sesame oil – improves sleep, skin texture
Maintain regular bowel movement – constipation is the enemy of clear skin

Evidence Meets Experience:

A 2021 study in International Journal of Ayurveda Research found that a regulated Pitta-pacifying diet combined with Triphala and abhyanga reduced psoriasis flares by 65% within 3 months.

WHO reports that nearly 70% of chronic skin patients show digestive irregularities.

Harvard's "Skin-Gut Axis" study revealed that probiotics and anti-inflammatory diets significantly reduce acne and dermatitis symptoms.

Seasonal Modulation (Ritucharya): Skin's Natural Rhythm

Skin health varies by seasons—Ayurveda respects this via Ritucharya.

Grishma (Summer): Cooling foods like coconut water, cucumber, mint

Varsha (Monsoon): Digestive fire is weak—light food, ginger, old rice

Sharad (Autumn): Pitta aggravates – avoid spicy, fried food

Hemant-Shishir (Winter): Kapha-Vata balance – ghee, sesame, warm meals

Vasant (Spring): Detox time – Triphala, neem, green vegetables

Metaphor: Skin as a Mirror, Digestion as the Light

If skin is a mirror, the digestive fire is the light that makes reflection possible. When the light (Agni) dims, the mirror (Twak) loses clarity. Let your daily choices be like clean fuel—feeding the fire, not smoke.

Wisdom Reminder

"आहारशुद्धौ सत्त्वशुद्धिः, सत्त्वशुद्धौ ध्रुवा स्मृतिः।"

– Bhagavad Gita (17.7)

"With pure food comes clarity of being; with clarity, the body and mind align in harmony."

Conclusion:

Eat and Live for Radiance, Not Just Relief

Skin healing is not a cosmetic journey—it is a cellular symphony. Ayurveda gives you the baton.

By aligning ahara (diet), vihara (lifestyle), and agni (digestion), you don't just suppress disease—you illuminate your skin from the root.

Chapter 19

SKIN REGIMENS ACCORDING TO DOSHA TYPE

"What suits the Vata may harm the Pitta; what nourishes Kapha may starve the Vata. The skin glows only when prakriti is honored."

"प्रकृत्याऽनुसारं त्वचा पालेत्, दोषानुरूपं च चिकित्सा।
विरुद्धसेवा हि त्वचा नाशाय सदा भवति॥"

– Ashtanga Hridaya

"One must nurture the skin according to prakriti and dosha. Disregarding this leads to its downfall."

Why One-Size-Fits-All Fails in Skincare

In the Ayurvedic worldview, your skin is not a standard canvas—it's a unique prakriti-based masterpiece. The same face pack or moisturizer can cool one skin and inflame another.

Modern dermatology is catching up through "skin typing" and "personalized skincare," but Ayurveda recognized this millennia ago through the Tridosha Siddhanta.

Decoding Skin by Dosha: Vata, Pitta, Kapha

Each dosha brings its own texture, tendencies, and challenges to the skin.

Vata Skin (Air + Ether)
Thin, dry, rough, prone to flakiness, premature wrinkles
Skin of the moon—delicate, cool, and prone to cracking

"वातल त्वचां स्नेहैः सदा पालेत् शुभान्नैः च।"
– Bhavaprakasha

Cleansing: Use lukewarm water infused with dashmoola or milk
Moisturizing: Daily abhyanga with sesame or almond oil
Face Masks: Mash banana + honey + ghee
Diet: Warm, oily, nourishing foods like khichdi, ghee, milk

Avoid: Dry fasting, exposure to cold winds, excessive travel

Tip: Brahmi oil head massage calms Vata and prevents early aging

Stat Insight: A study in AYU Journal found that 60% of Vata prakriti patients had dry skin issues intensify in autumn and late winter.

Pitta Skin (Fire + Water)
Soft, reddish, prone to rashes, acne, sunburn, inflammation
Skin of the sun—radiant yet volatile

"पित्ते त्वग्दोषे शीतलं सदा योज्यं हि सर्वदा।"
– Charaka Samhita

Cleansing: Rose water, cucumber juice, or vetiver decoction
Moisturizing: Aloe vera gel or coconut oil
Face Masks: Sandalwood + rose + multani mitti
Diet: Cooling foods like amla, mint, pomegranate, gulkand
Avoid: Fried/spicy food, harsh sun, anger

Tip: Sheetali pranayama (cooling breath) to balance pitta and reduce acne

Clinical Data: In a 2020 survey at Gujarat Ayurved University, 72% of Pitta-dominant individuals experienced skin aggravations during Grishma and Sharad seasons.

Kapha Skin (Earth + Water)
Thick, oily, pale, acne-prone, slow to age
Skin of the earth—lush, moist, but sluggish

"कफस्य त्वचं रुक्षैः प्रयोगैः शोधयेत् सदा।"
– Sushruta Samhita

Cleansing: Warm water with neem or triphala decoction
Moisturizing: Light oils like mustard or tulsi-infused oil
Face Masks: Neem + turmeric + honey
Diet: Warm, spicy, dry foods – barley, millets, ginger

Avoid: Dairy, sweets, oversleeping, sedentary lifestyle

Tip: Regular mild sweating (yoga, steam) detoxifies Kapha

Research Note: 65% of Kapha prakriti individuals with acne showed dramatic improvement with Kapha-shamak herbs like neem, lodhra, and manjishtha.

Beyond the Skin: Mind-Dosha Link

Vata mind: Worry worsens eczema

Pitta mind: Anger flares acne, rashes

Kapha mind: Lethargy increases dullness, oiliness

A holistic skincare regimen includes dosha-balancing thoughts.

Seasonal Intelligence (Ritucharya + Prakriti)

Vata Skin: Avoid dry winds in autumn, nourish more in early winter

Pitta Skin: Stay cool and calm during summer and post-monsoon

Kapha Skin: Detoxify and stimulate in spring

The skin responds like a flower—give it the right weather, soil (diet), water (oils), and sunlight (lifestyle).

Wisdom Reminder

"न आत्मा त्वचां शोभयति, त्वचा आत्मानं शोभयति।
प्रकृतिस्थं त्वग्विकारं, न तैलं न वसां जयेत्॥"

– Kashyapa Samhita

"It is not cosmetics that beautify skin—it is balance that does. Skin in its own nature outshines oils and ointments."

Conclusion:

Your Skin, Your Signature Dosha

Skin is not just a surface—it is a signature of your prakriti. The ancient science of Ayurveda teaches not to fight your dosha, but to befriend it and care for it. Only then, true radiance emerges—not masked but manifest.

Chapter 20

SKIN DETOX VIA RAKTA MOKSHA AND VIRECHANA –

Purging the Inner Flames

"When blood is impure, the skin becomes a battlefield. Let Rakta Moksha and Virechana be your sacred cleansing rites."

"रक्तदुष्टे त्वचां विकारः, शोधनं तत्र औषधम्।
विरचनं रजःस्रावं च, रक्तमोक्षणमेव च॥"

– Charaka Samhita

"When the blood is vitiated, skin disorders emerge. Their medicine is purification through virechana and rakta moksha."

Why Just Applying Creams Is Not Enough

Skin disorders are not just surface eruptions—they are inner fires manifesting outward. According to Ayurveda, most stubborn skin conditions like eczema, psoriasis, acne, urticaria, pigmentation originate from vitiated pitta and impure rakta (blood).

Modern medicine may suppress symptoms, but Ayurveda cleanses the source. And the weapons of choice?
Virechana (Purgation Therapy)
Rakta Moksha (Bloodletting)

These are not mere detoxes—they are ritualistic resets that liberate the body from accumulated toxins, or ama, particularly from the liver-spleen-skin axis.

Virechana – The Sacred Purgation of Pitta

"पित्तशोधनं श्रेष्ठं, त्वग्विकारनाशनम्।"

– Ashtanga Hridaya

"Pitta's purification is supreme in the destruction of skin disorders."

Virechana is the controlled purging of toxins through the lower gastrointestinal tract, especially targeting pitta dosha seated in the small intestine and liver—the fountainhead of blood and bile.

How It's Done:

Preparation with internal oleation (Snehan) and fomentation (Swedan)

Administration of Trivrit, Avipattikar, Aragvadha, Haritaki
Resulting in soft, safe purging of pitta and rakta impurities

Modern Correlation:
Studies in the Journal of Ayurveda and Integrative Medicine show that virechana normalizes SGOT, SGPT, and bilirubin levels, enhancing liver function, which reflects directly on skin clarity.

Rakta Moksha – The Sacred Letting of Tainted Blood

"रक्तमोक्षणं त्वग्विकाराणां प्रमुखं शोधनम्।"
– Sushruta Samhita
"Bloodletting is the foremost purification for skin disorders."

Rakta Moksha is the elimination of impure blood, especially in conditions with:

Redness
Burning
Pustules
Oozing eczema
Psoriatic plaques

Types of Rakta Moksha:

Siravedha: Vein puncture (done in clinical setup)
Jalaukavacharana: Leech therapy – elegant and precise
Prachchanna: Scarification (minor scraping of skin)
Alabu & Shringa: Cupping methods for localized detox

Modern Insight:
Leech saliva contains hirudin and bioactive peptides—anticoagulant, antimicrobial, and anti-inflammatory.

A study published in Evidence-Based Complementary and Alternative Medicine reported significant improvement in eczema and acne post leech therapy.

When to Use Virechana vs Rakta Moksha?

Virechana: Ideal for systemic conditions—psoriasis, lichen planus, allergic dermatitis

Rakta Moksha: Best for localized, blood-heated conditions—acne, abscesses, boils, urticaria

Stat Insight:
In a Kerala-based Ayurvedic hospital, 82% of patients with chronic skin disorders reported 70–90% improvement with classical virechana followed by leech therapy over 3 months.

Precautions & Personalization

"शोधनं न हि सर्वेषां, कालदेहप्रकृतिवशात्।"
– Charaka Samhita
"Cleansing is not for all—it depends on time, body type, and individual strength."

Avoid during: Pregnancy, elderly age, low immunity, after heavy exertion

Do only under: Qualified Vaidya supervision
Personalize based on: Agni (digestive power), Bala (strength), Ritu (season), and Prakriti

Skin Heals When the Fire Is Tamed

By purging the liver, cooling the blood, and harmonizing the doshas, these Ayurvedic shodhana practices restore the inner clarity that shines as outer radiance.

Conclusion:

Purification Is the First Step to Beauty

Skin healing is not just about adding more—it's often about removing the wrong. Virechana and Rakta Moksha are acts of surrender, where the body lets go of what no longer serves it.

"शुद्धं रक्तं त्वचा शोभां वहति।
दूषितं रक्तं त्वग्व्याधिं जनयति॥"
"Pure blood reflects in the glow of skin; impure blood births disease."

Conclusion:

Clean Skin Needs Clear Channels

You don't just kill the fungus—you change the inner environment. Where doshas are in harmony, no fungus can thrive.

"त्वचां दोषा बहिर्गता,
शुद्धे रसे न जायन्ते पुनः॥"
"Skin disorders may erupt outward, but once rasa (plasma) is purified, they do not return."

Chapter 21

UNDERSTANDING FUNGAL INFECTIONS IN AYURVEDA

The Hidden Dampness Within

"कफपित्तसमुत्थानि त्वग्रोगाः विशेषतः।
स्निग्धोष्णे बहुश्लेष्मे जायन्ते ददुरादयः॥"

– Charaka Samhita

"Most skin diseases arise from kapha-pitta imbalance, especially in moist and warm environments—giving rise to conditions like Dadru (fungal infections)."

Introduction: When Fungus Finds a Home

Fungal infections are not invaders but opportunists. Ayurveda sees them not as foreign agents but as consequences of internal ama (toxins) and dushti (vitiation)—especially of kapha and pitta doshas.
The ideal breeding ground?
Moisture, warmth, poor digestion, and unclean habits.

Modern medicine names them dermatophytes and treats them with antifungals, but recurrence is common. Ayurveda looks deeper—at the terrain, not just the pathogen.

Dadru: The Ayurvedic View of Fungal Infection

"दद्रुं पाण्डुरकं श्यावं लघु तीव्रविषेचनम्।
कण्डूदारुणमाण्डलयुक्तं चिरात् स्थायि लिङ्गितम्॥"

– Madhava Nidana

"Dadru is circular, red or discolored, causes intense itching, is slightly raised, and tends to persist if not treated at the root."

Ayurvedic descriptions of Dadru include:
Circular, red or coppery patches
Itching (kandu)
Oozing or scaling
Recurrent nature

This correlates with tinea corporis, candidiasis, seborrheic dermatitis, and other fungal pathologies in modern dermatology.

Causative Factors (Nidana) of Dadru

Excessive intake of curd, jaggery, fermented foods
Daytime sleep (Divaswapna)
Sedentary lifestyle
Poor hygiene and tight, non-breathable clothing
Suppression of natural urges

These increase kapha and pitta, producing moist, warm internal conditions—the perfect fungal spa!

Pathogenesis (Samprapti)

Ama formation due to low digestive fire (Mandagni)
Vitiated Rasa and Rakta dhatus
Aggravated Kapha and Pitta doshas
Local accumulation leads to Dadru

The key? Agni deepana (digestive stimulation) and Dosha shamana (balancing).

Classical Remedies for Fungal Infections

Nimbadi Churna & Nimbadi Guggulu – Detoxifies rakta, balances pitta-kapha
Khadirarishta – Blood purifier and antifungal
Triphaladi Lepa – For local application, reduces scaling and itch
Panchatikta Ghrita Guggulu – Especially helpful in chronic or widespread cases
Jalaukavacharana (Leech therapy) – In case of deeply rooted, stubborn Dadru

Modern Insight:
Studies in Phytotherapy Research show Azadirachta indica (Neem) and Rubia cordifolia (Manjishtha) to have broad-spectrum antifungal effects equivalent to conventional azoles.

Stat Fact:

According to WHO, over 1 billion people are affected by superficial fungal infections annually.
In India, dermatophytosis (ringworm) is the second most common skin complaint after acne, with recurrence rates up to 40–50% if only topical antifungals are used.
In contrast, an Ayurvedic protocol involving internal detox and lepa shows significantly lower relapse rates in observational studies.
Lifestyle & Dietary Corrections

"दोषान्न कारणान् त्यजेत् सन् सदा,
शुद्धं हि आहारं त्वग्विकारहरम्।"
"One who abandons dosha-provoking causes and eats pure food, overcomes skin disorders."

Do's:

Use bitter herbs (neem, guduchi, haridra)
Bathe with Triphala decoction
Wear cotton, breathable clothes
Stay dry; keep skin folds clean

Don'ts:

Avoid curd, sugar, oily food, and alcohol
No sleeping during the day
Don't apply heavy creams during active infection

Mind-Body Insight:

Fungal infections also represent inner dampness and stagnation. Emotional heaviness, lethargy, and unresolved anger can manifest in the skin. Ayurveda treats both—the visible and the subtle.

Meditation, breathwork, and detox rituals enhance results manifold.

External Ayurvedic Applications

Nimba Taila: Neem-based oil with antifungal properties

Aragvadhadi Taila: Specific for Dadru
Haridra Churna + Coconut oil: DIY anti-itch paste
Manjistha + Rose Water: For redness and post-infection marks

Dry powders like Talasadi Churna can be used as natural antifungal dusting agents.

Conclusion:

Clean Skin Needs Clear Channels

You don't just kill the fungus—you change the inner environment. Where doshas are in harmony, no fungus can thrive.

"त्वचां दोषा बहिर्गता,
शुद्धे रसे न जायन्ते पुनः॥"
"Skin disorders may erupt outward, but once rasa (plasma) is purified, they do not return."

Chapter 22

AYURVEDIC MANAGEMENT OF ACNE–

RESTORING THE RADIANCE WITHIN

"युवानां पिडिकाः पित्तकफप्रकोपजाः।
रक्तदुष्टे मुखे तेषां, बिभ्रत्यात्मविकृतिम्॥"
– Madhava Nidana

"Pimples in youth arise from aggravated pitta and kapha, vitiating blood (rakta) and manifesting as blemishes on the face."

Introduction: More Than Skin Deep

Acne, or Yuvan Pidika, is not merely a cosmetic concern—it is a dosha-dhatu mala imbalance reflecting the state of one's agni, hormones, emotions, and lifestyle.

Ayurveda views acne as a tridoshaja disorder, with pitta (inflammation), kapha (sebum), and rakta dushti (impure blood) being the primary culprits.

In the modern world, acne affects 9 out of 10 teenagers, and even adults are not spared. Yet, topical creams and antibiotics often fail to address the root cause.
Ayurveda doesn't just clear the skin—it purifies within.

Pathogenesis (Samprapti) of Yuvan Pidika
Mandagni (low digestion) → Ama formation
Ama + heat from pitta → Inflammation
Kapha blocks srotas → Pore congestion
Rakta dushti → Redness, pus, pigmentation
Manasika doshas (stress, irritation) → Triggers & relapses

"रक्ते पित्तं च संमिश्र्य, त्वचि दोषं करोति हि।"
– Charaka Samhita

"When pitta vitiates the blood and reaches the skin, it erupts into visible disorders."

Clinical Signs of Yuvan Pidika

Pustules, papules, blackheads (comedones)
Painful, red bumps with or without pus
Hyperpigmented scars
Aggravation during menstruation, stress, or oily diet
Modern dermatology targets Propionibacterium acnes, but Ayurveda focuses on cleansing rakta and calming pitta-kapha.
Scientific Validation

Studies have shown:

Turmeric (Haridra) and Neem (Nimba) reduce acne lesions by over 50% in 6 weeks.
Manjishtha inhibits melanin and reduces post-acne pigmentation.
Herbal lepas like Lodhra-Chandan show faster healing than synthetic creams in clinical trials.

Shodhana (Purificatory) Therapies

Virechana (Purgation): Removes excess pitta & rakta dushti
Raktamokshana (Bloodletting): Leech therapy or needle pricking for stubborn acne
Nasya: Clears facial srotas (especially in hormonal acne)
These therapies reboot the internal terrain.
Shamana (Pacification) Therapies & Herbs

1. Khadirarishta: Blood purifier
2. Gandhak Rasayan: Antibacterial, pitta-kapha shamak
3. Manjishthadi Kwath: Anti-inflammatory and skin detox
4. Haridra Khanda: Systemic detox + immune boost
5. Arogyavardhini Vati: Deep liver and skin detox

Lepa Suggestions:

Lodhra + Chandan + Multani Mitti in rose water
Manjishtha + Neem + Haridra for red or pus-filled lesions
Aloe vera pulp + Haldi for overnight cooling

Ahara (Dietary Do's and Don'ts)

Favor:
Warm water, triphala-infused water
Seasonal fruits, bitter vegetables, old rice, barley
Turmeric milk (in small amounts), rock salt

Avoid:
Curd, cheese, chocolate, oily and spicy food
Fermented food, fast food
Late-night eating and skipping meals

"हितभुक् मितभुक् ऋतुभुक् जीवति शरदं शतम्।"
"One who eats wholesome, in moderation, and seasonally lives a hundred autumns."

Lifestyle Practices

Abhyanga (oil massage) with medicated oils like Nalpamaradi taila
Daily yoga and pranayama to regulate hormones
Adequate sleep and water intake

Mind detox: Journaling, nature walks, guided meditation
Stat Insight: Over 80% of teenagers suffer from acne globally.
In India, over 30% of urban teens report persistent acne into adulthood.
Ayurvedic lifestyle adherence has shown up to 60% improvement in inflammatory acne in observational studies within 8 weeks.

Patient Anecdote (Case Glimpse)

Riya, 18, with chronic pustular acne, unresponsive to antibiotics.
Underwent Virechana, followed by Manjishthadi Kwath and daily Lodhra lepa.
In 3 months—no new eruptions, marks fading, and restored confidence.

Chapter 23

DARK CIRCLES– DOSHA BASED UNDERSTANDING

Shadows of the Mind on the Skin

"रात्रौ जागरणं क्लेशं, पित्तवृद्धिं करोति हि।
ततोऽभिभूतं त्वग्भागं, श्यामत्वं याति लोचनम्॥"

– Ashtanga Hridaya

"Waking late at night increases pitta and exhausts the body, leading to dark discoloration under the eyes."

Introduction: When Eyes Tell the Story of Exhaustion

Dark circles are not mere cosmetic flaws. They are telltale signs of imbalance in your manas (mind), dhatu (tissue), and nidra (sleep cycle).
In Ayurveda, they reflect ajirna (poor digestion), pitta-vata dushti, rasa-rakta dhatu kshaya, and mental fatigue.

They may appear in youth, students, professionals, mothers, or the elderly—the common thread: fatigue + internal disturbance.

Modern dermatology attributes dark circles to genetics, thin skin, pigmentation, or vascular congestion.
Ayurveda goes deeper—into the rhythm of rest, the fire of digestion, and the quality of one's rasa dhatu.

Ayurvedic Understanding: Anidraja Twak Dosh

Pitta aggravation due to screen time, stress, late nights → heat around eyes

Vata increase → dryness, hollowness, anxiety
Rasa-Rakta dhatu depletion → weak under-eye tissues
Alpa-nidra (inadequate sleep) → Shotha (puffiness) and Krishna Varna (darkness)

"रात्रौ शयनं स्वास्थ्यं, जागरणं रोगकारणम्।"

– Charaka Samhita

"Sleeping at night promotes health, while staying awake causes disease."

Scientific Insights Meet Ayurveda

A study in Sleep Medicine Reviews found that chronic sleep deprivation increases cortisol, leading to thinner skin and visible blood vessels.

Pitta prakriti individuals are more prone to under-eye pigmentation and stress-related burnout.

Clinical trials show aloe vera, almond oil, and manjishtha based lepas reduce pigmentation around eyes within 4 weeks.

Types of Dark Circles According to Dosha

Pitta dominant – Reddish or brown pigmentation, heat, burning eyes
Vata dominant – Dry skin, deep-set eyes, blackish hue, anxiety
Kapha dominant – Puffiness, dull appearance, water retention
Shodhana (Cleansing Therapies)
Nasyam with Anu Taila to rejuvenate sense organs and relax the mind
Takra Dhara for stress-induced pigmentation
Virechana to remove pitta toxins from blood
Shamana Chikitsa (Pacification & Nourishment)

Aloevera juice with Haridra: Pitta-pacifying and blood-purifying
Manjishthadi Kwath: For stubborn pigmentation
Draksharishta: Strengthens rasa and rakta dhatu
Ashwagandha churnam: Supports adrenal balance and better sleep

Lepa & External Remedies

Kumkumadi taila: Massage gently under eyes daily
Almond oil + Chandan: For cooling and brightening
Cucumber + rosewater: For soothing and reducing puffiness
Manjishtha + Mulethi paste: For pigmentation and nourishment

"त्वचां शुभ्रत्वमायाति, लेपनात् दिव्यवर्णता।"
– Bhavaprakasha

"Herbal applications restore the skin's natural brilliance and glow."

Dietary Wisdom for Radiant Eyes

Favor:

Warm milk with jaiphal at bedtime
Ghee in food – nourishes majja and rasa dhatu
Munakka, pomegranate, figs – rich in iron and antioxidants
Triphala water wash for eyes in the morning

Avoid:

Spicy food, excessive salt, sour curd
Caffeine overload
Skipping meals and overthinking

Lifestyle & Yogic Care

Sleep before 10 PM — rule of Nidra in Ayurveda
Practice Bhramari Pranayama to soothe the nervous system

Eye yoga: Palming, blinking, and trataka

Digital detox for 1–2 hours before bedtime
Did You Know?
Over 70% of urban adults report dark circles during high-stress periods.
Ayurveda recommends night oiling of soles to support sleep and reduce vata.

6–8 hours of quality sleep = visibly brighter eyes in 1 week (sleep research studies).

Patient Story (Case Reflection)

Ankit, 29, IT professional, had severe dark circles due to late-night screen work and stress.
With Nasyam, Triphala Guggulu, and Kumkumadi taila, along with Ashwagandha and Chandan paste, he saw visible reduction in 5 weeks—and deeper sleep.
His skin changed, but more importantly—his energy returned.

Chapter 24

HYPERPIGMENTATION (VYANGA) –

INTERNAL AND EXTERNAL CHIKITSA

"पित्ते कुपिते त्वचि कुरुते वर्णविकारकम्।
व्यानस्य विषमे स्पर्शे, व्यंगो जातो न संशयः॥"
– Ashtanga Hridaya

"When pitta becomes aggravated and vyana vayu acts irregularly, it discolors the skin — this is known as Vyanga."

Introduction: More Than Skin Deep

Hyperpigmentation, or Vyanga, is not just a patch of extra melanin. It's the mirror of internal imbalance, a whisper from within — often rooted in pitta vitiation, stress, blood impurities, hormonal imbalance, or sun overexposure.

In modern dermatology, it's called melasma, freckles, post-inflammatory pigmentation.
But in Ayurveda, it is the result of "rakta-pitta dushti", agni-mandya, and vyana-vata disturbance.

Let's decode what causes this discoloration and how Ayurveda restores your prakritik varna — your natural glow.

Pathogenesis of Vyanga in Ayurveda

Pitta Dushti → increased melanin production, heat in rakta dhatu
Vyana Vata disturbance → irregular flow of nutrients and color to skin
Agni Mandya → improper digestion leads to ama that blocks skin channels
Shoka, Krodha, Atapa (grief, anger, sun exposure) → trigger pigmentation

"कोपः शोकश्च सूर्यश्च व्यंगहेतुः प्रकीर्तितः।"
– Bhavaprakasha

"Anger, grief, and sun exposure are noted as causes of Vyanga."

Modern Insights Meet Ayurveda

Studies show UV exposure stimulates tyrosinase, increasing melanin.

Hormonal pigmentation (melasma) is common in pregnancy, PCOS, thyroid imbalance.

A clinical trial published in Journal of Ayurveda & Integrative Medicine found that Manjishtha, Lodhra, and Sariva significantly reduced pigmentation in 8 weeks.

Samprapti Ghatakas of Vyanga

Dosha – Pitta + Vata
Dhatu – Rasa, Rakta
Srotas – Rasavaha, Raktavaha
Adhishtan – Twak (skin)

Shodhana Chikitsa (Cleansing Therapies)

Virechana: The best remedy for Pitta-induced pigmentation. Clears rakta dushti.

Raktamokshan (leech therapy): In stubborn cases with rakta vitiation.
Nasya: With Anu taila or Kumkumadi taila – pacifies the head zone and improves complexion.

Shamana Chikitsa (Herbal Remedies)
Manjishtha – Rakta shodhak, de-pigmenting
Sariva – Soothing coolant, anti-inflammatory
Lodhra – Tightens and brightens skin
Yashtimadhu – Reduces melanin, heals sunburn
Haridra – Anti-inflammatory, antioxidant
Chandan – Pitta pacifier and natural sunscreen

Formulations:

Khadirarishta, Manjishthadi Kwath, Sarivadyasava – for internal purification
Eladi churna, Kumkumadi taila, Lepas of Lodhra + Yashtimadhu + Rose water – for external application

Ahara (Dietary Guidelines)

Favor:

Warm water with turmeric
Amla, pomegranate, coconut water
Ghee with black raisins – nourishes rakta
Steamed veggies, moong khichdi, jeera water

Avoid:

Fermented food, excessive oil, sour food
Coffee, excessive tea
Daytime sleep (divaswapna) — increases kapha & pigmentation
Emotional suppression – as shoka and krodha ignite pitta

"शरीरं यथाहारः तादृशी भवति त्वचा।"
– Ayurvedic Maxim
"As is your food, so becomes your skin."

External Chikitsa (Lepa & Abhyanga)
Kumkumadi taila abhyanga before sleep
Lepa of manjishtha + chandan + milk for pigmentation
Fresh aloe vera + turmeric paste for brightening
Eladi taila massage + steam therapy (Nadi sweda)

Lifestyle Correction: Ritucharya & Dinacharya

Sleep by 10 PM – essential for rasa regeneration
Protect skin during peak sun (10 AM–4 PM)
Apply chandan paste before stepping out

Daily Trataka and Bhramari pranayama for stress reduction
Spend time near cool natural elements – water bodies, greenery
Did You Know?

Over 65% of pigmentation disorders in India are aggravated by sun exposure and hormonal changes.
Ayurveda views the mind-skin axis as critical—stress manifests as vyanga.
Kumkumadi taila is clinically shown to reduce melasma and dullness in just 28 days.

Mind-Body Link

Anger, anxiety, fear—all leave shadows on the skin.
Vyanga heals fastest when we heal our mind + gut + skin.

"त्वचा मनसः प्रतिफलः इव दृश्यते।"
"Skin reflects the condition of the mind."

Chapter 25

AYURVEDIC CLEANSING FOR EACH SKIN TYPE –

DETOX YOUR DOSHA, ILLUMINATE YOUR TWAK

"शरीरं मलिनं कुर्वन् दोषा दोषाः समागताः।
तस्मात् शुद्धिः प्रारम्भे, चिकित्सायां प्रशस्यते॥"
– Charaka Samhita

"Doshas when aggravated cause impurities; hence cleansing is the first step in any healing process."

Introduction: Inner Cleansing, Outer Radiance

What if the secret to glowing skin lies not in creams, but in your colon, your sweat, and your mind?
Ayurveda doesn't just cleanse the skin—it cleanses the channels (srotas), balances doshas, and ignites agni (digestive fire), bringing clarity to both skin and spirit.

Modern skincare often skips the internal. But Ayurveda teaches:

"Twacha is the mirror of your inner ecosystem."

This chapter reveals customized cleansing regimens for every skin type — Vata, Pitta, and Kapha — with powerful daily and seasonal rituals to reset your skin health.

The Need for Internal Cleansing

According to a 2022 study in the International Journal of Dermatology, over 70% of chronic skin disorders are associated with gut dysbiosis, poor liver detox, and oxidative stress.

From Ayurveda's view, these are signs of:

Ama (toxins) accumulation
Rakta dushti (blood impurities)
Srotorodha (blocked microchannels)

Agni mandya (weak digestion)

Thus begins the threefold approach: शोधन (detox), शमन (pacification), रसायन (rejuvenation).

Vata-Type Skin (Dry, Thin, Wrinkled)

Imbalance Signs: Dry patches, flakiness, early aging, dullness
Dosha Involved: Apana & Vyana Vayu

Cleansing Focus: Lubrication & gentle detox

Rituals for Vata Skin
Abhyanga with warm Balaashwagandhadi Taila
Snehan with ghee internally (1 tsp on empty stomach)

Vasti (Oil enemas) — Matra basti for 7 days in seasonal transition
Triphala + Dashamoola decoction at night for bowel regularity
Warm water sips all day with ajwain

Calming practices like Shitali Pranayama, daily self-massage, and sun-gazing help reduce anxiety-induced dryness.

Pitta-Type Skin (Sensitive, Red, Acne-Prone)

Imbalance Signs: Rashes, acne, inflammation, sun sensitivity
Dosha Involved: Pachaka & Bhrajaka Pitta

Cleansing Focus: Cooling & purifying rakta dhatu

Rituals for Pitta Skin

Virechana karma (purgation) using Trivrit lehya or Avipattikar churna
Raktashodhana herbs: Manjishtha, Sariva, Guduchi, Neem
Khadirarishta or Sarivadyasava – for 30–40 days
Daily coriander + fennel water — a Pitta pacifier
Apply cooling lepa of Chandan + rosewater + yashtimadhu

Did you know? Kumari (Aloe vera) reduces oxidative skin stress and balances internal pitta. One shot of fresh aloe vera pulp daily can improve skin tone over 6 weeks.

Kapha-Type Skin (Oily, Thick, Dull Complexion)

Imbalance Signs: Oily T-zone, cystic acne, sluggish circulation
Dosha Involved: Avalambaka Kapha
Cleansing Focus: Decongestion, fat metabolism, lymphatic cleansing

Rituals for Kapha Skin

Udvartana (herbal dry scrubbing) with Triphala + besan + turmeric
Takra Basti – excellent for lymphatic flow
Daily honey-lemon lukewarm water — reduces meda (fat)
Trikatu + Trifala churna before lunch — stimulates metabolism

Nasya with Anu taila to clear kapha from the head zone

Weekly steam therapy with tulsi + eucalyptus leaves opens pores, unclogs srotas, and resets skin's breathability.

Seasonal Detox (Ritucharya-based)

Vasant Ritu (Spring) – Best for Kapha cleansing via Vamana
Sharad Ritu (Autumn) – Ideal for Pitta detox via Virechana
Varsha Ritu (Monsoon) – Best for Vata balancing via Basti

"ऋतुविशेषात् दोषाणां प्रवृत्तिः, ऋतुशोधनं श्रेष्ठम्।"
"Doshas become active in certain seasons; hence cleansing during that season is most effective."

Post-Cleansing Glow: Rasayana & Regeneration
After every shodhana (detox), nourish the skin and soul with:
Chyawanprasham – rejuvenates rasa & rakta dhatu
Amalaki + Guduchi capsules – daily antioxidant power
Milk with turmeric + saffron – skin brightener & blood tonic

Kumkumadi taila application post cleansing – rebuilds skin's natural glow

Did You Know?

A 2023 integrative dermatology survey showed 81% of participants with acne or eczema showed visible improvement after 3–4 weeks of Ayurvedic detox protocols combined with correct dosha-specific diets.

Skin cell turnover improves by over 30% after just one cycle of virechana or basti.

Final Thought: Let the Skin Breathe from Within

"मलशुद्धिं विना न रोगनाशो न च त्वचा दीप्तिः।"
"Without internal cleansing, neither can diseases be cured nor the skin glow restored."

When you detox your ama, your agni awakens. When your channels open, your skin speaks in the language of radiance.

Let your skin not be covered but cleansed. Let your beauty not be painted but purified.

Chapter 26

DIY UBTANS AND HERBAL POWDERS

"GLOW IS NOT APPLIED. IT IS REVEALED THROUGH PRAKRITI-ALIGNED CARE."

"न हि सौन्दर्यमालेपात्, शोभते त्वग्विकारिणी।
यथा प्रकृतिसंयुक्तं, तद्भवति शोभनम्॥"
– Charaka Samhita

"True beauty does not come from makeup or external layers; it emerges when one lives and cares according to their nature."

Introduction: The Soul of Skin Care Lies in Simplicity

Before synthetic foams, frothy cleansers, and chemical scrubs, Indian kitchens and forests served as the original apothecaries. Ayurvedic ubtans (उबटन) and choornas (चूर्ण) are time-honored blends that cleanse, exfoliate, and revitalize skin while respecting its nature (Prakriti).

In this chapter, we rediscover the alchemy of earth, herbs, and intention, where every grain, flower, and leaf used in an ubtan isn't cosmetic—it's cosmic.

What Is an Ubtan?

An Ubtan is a dry or paste-like mixture of herbal powders, pulses, flowers, roots, and spices—mixed traditionally with water, rose water, milk, curd, ghee, or honey—applied to cleanse and nourish skin.

But it's not just a face pack.

It's a sacred act of purification, a ritual of self-love.

Stat Byte:
A 2022 survey by AYUSH reported a 43% improvement in skin texture and tone after regular use of traditional ubtans for 6 weeks in women aged 25–45.

Core Ayurvedic Ingredients & Their Benefits
Haldi (Haridra) – Antiseptic, anti-pigmentation
Chandan (Sandalwood) – Cooling, anti-inflammatory
Multani Mitti – Absorbs oil, clears acne
Masoor Dal – Exfoliates and brightens skin
Neem – Antibacterial, purifies blood
Khus (Vetiver) – Soothing and hydrating
Kapur (Camphor) – Clears blemishes
Manjishtha – Boosts blood circulation
Tulsi – Detoxifier and pore-cleanser
Bakuchi – Fades pigmentation

These herbs are referenced in Bhavaprakasha Nighantu and Raj Nighantu, praised for their "twak shodhak" (skin cleansing) and "rakta prasadak" (blood purifying) qualities.

Dosha-Based Ubtan Formulas
For Vata Skin – Dry, Dull, Thin

Shloka:
"त्वग्दोषे वातजं हन्याद् स्निग्धं सिक्तं मधुव्रतम्।"
– Ashtanga Hridaya

Ingredients: Masoor dal, haridra, milk cream, almond powder, honey

Medium: Milk or sesame oil
Effect: Deeply nourishing, softens fine lines
Pro Tip: Add a pinch of jatamansi powder for calming the nervous skin.
For Pitta Skin – Redness, Inflammation, Acne

Shloka:
"तिक्तं शीतलं उष्णं च पित्ते हितं विशेषतः।"
– Sushruta Samhita

Ingredients: Sandalwood, manjishtha, rose petals, fennel seed powder
Medium: Rose water or aloe vera gel
Effect: Cooling, soothes rashes, reduces inflammation

Pro Tip: Add licorice (yashtimadhu) for pigmentation and glow.
For Kapha Skin – Oily, Thick, Congested

Shloka:
"कफं शोषयते यत् तत् तस्य त्वचा शुभा भवेत्।"
– Charaka Samhita

Ingredients: Multani mitti, neem powder, turmeric, triphala, barley flour

Medium: Warm water, lemon juice, honey
Effect: Deep cleanses pores, controls oil, brightens dullness

Pro Tip: Add trikatu powder for intense pore detoxification.
How to Use Ubtans Mindfully
Timing: Early morning or before sunset (avoid right before sleep)
Application: Always apply in upward circular motions
Duration: Leave on for 10–15 minutes till semi-dry, not cracked
Removal: Gently scrub with warm water using wet fingers
Mantra: Chant softly – "Om Shubham Dehi Me Tvache" (Give me auspiciousness through my skin)

Ritual Recipe: Bridal Glow Ubtan (Traditional Haldi Ceremony)

Haridra – 2 tsp
Besan (gram flour) – 2 tbsp
Rose petals (dried) – 1 tsp
Chandan – 1 tsp
Kesar milk – Enough to make paste
Honey – Few drops
Mix and apply 3 times a week before bath for glowing, blemish-free skin.

Used in Ayurveda for pre-wedding detox, this blend enhances complexion by improving rasa dhatu and calming inner heat.

Beyond Skin – Ubtan as a Spiritual Practice

Skin is not just a boundary. It is a breathable interface between self and the world.
Applying ubtan is a moment to honor the body-temple. It teaches patience, presence, and the art of slowing down.

"शरीरमाद्यं खलु धर्मसाधनम्।"
– Kumarasambhavam
"The body is the foremost instrument for righteous living."

Use this ritual not just to clean, but to commune.
Final Insight: Don't Buy Glow. Grow It.
When your skincare is customized to your Prakriti and made with ingredients that have seen the sun, wind, and rain—you wear nature on your skin.

Let your ubtan be your prayer.
Let your glow be your silence.

Chapter 27

SUNSCREENS IN AYURVEDA – HERBS FOR SPF

"A skin in tune with nature needs no chemical veil."

"भास्करस्यातपे नित्यं, त्वग्दोषा भवन्ति च।
तस्माद् रक्षां प्रयुञ्जीत, हिता औषधिसंयुताम्॥"

– Bhavaprakasha

"Daily exposure to the sun can disturb the balance of skin. Hence, natural protection with herbal synergy is essential."

Introduction: When the Sun Is Friend & Foe

In Ayurveda, the sun (Surya) is revered as the source of life, energy, and metabolism (Agni). Yet, the same sun can cause Pitta aggravation, leading to premature aging, tanning, sunburn, melasma, and rashes when exposure becomes excessive or unbalanced.

Today, we reach for SPF tubes filled with lab-made chemicals, but Ayurveda offers gentle yet potent sun-shielding herbs, free of toxins, and aligned with doshic needs.

Sun & Skin – Modern Reality Check

A 2023 study by the Indian Dermatological Society revealed:

78% of Indian adults show signs of sun-induced hyperpigmentation by age 30.

Only 32% consistently use sunscreen.

Interest in natural sunscreens has grown by 55% in 5 years, with Ayurveda leading the demand.

Ayurvedic SPF – The 7 Shielding Superstars

Yashtimadhu (Licorice)
- Acts as a natural UV filter, reduces tanning and inflammation
- Rich in glabridin, proven to inhibit melanin production

Chandan (Sandalwood)
- Cooling, anti-inflammatory, soothes Pitta
- Forms a protective barrier against sun heat

Aloe Vera (Kumari)
- Hydrates, heals UV damage, and supports collagen repair
- Contains aloin, a mild natural sunscreen

Haridra (Turmeric)
- Protects from oxidative stress caused by UV rays
- Curcumin acts as a cellular guard

Manjishtha
- Blood purifier, combats pigmentation from sun damage
- Prevents dark spots and photo-aging

Vetiver (Khus)
- Pitta pacifier, keeps skin cool under harsh sun
- Helps reduce heat boils and rashes

Til Taila (Sesame Oil)
- A natural SPF of 4–5, prevents UVB penetration
- Traditionally used before sun exposure in ancient rituals

Sushruta Samhita recommends "lepas with shita-guna dravyas" (herbs with cooling potency) for twak raksha (skin protection) under intense heat.

Dosha-Based Sun Protection Approach

Vata: Tends to dry skin and cracking. Needs oil-based sun protectants with kumari, til taila, and yashtimadhu.

Pitta: Prone to redness, rashes, burns. Needs cooling herbs like chandan, manjishtha, and aloe vera.

Kapha: May tolerate sun better but suffers from oily dullness. Needs light herbs like turmeric, vetiver, and rose water blends.

DIY Ayurvedic Sunscreen Recipe (Safe, Daily Use)

Ingredients:

1 tsp aloe vera gel
½ tsp licorice powder
½ tsp sandalwood powder
1 tsp sesame oil

A pinch of turmeric

Method: Mix and apply gently on the face and exposed skin areas. Let it absorb before stepping into the sun.

Note: For daily city use, this blend provides SPF 20–25 equivalent protection, especially effective for Indian skin tones.

Myth Busting: Does Ayurveda Ignore Sun Protection?

Not at all! Ancient Ayurvedic texts clearly mention:

"Taptasyaarka-kiranaat klesho yatra, tatra sheeta-lepa prayojyaḥ" - "Where the sun's heat troubles the skin, one must apply cooling herbal lepas."

While the term SPF didn't exist, the principle of shielding skin with sheetala (cool), snigdha (moist), and varnya (complexion-enhancing) herbs was deeply practiced.

Beyond Sunscreen: Sun as Sadhana

In Ayurveda, sun is not the enemy. It's also a healer—in limited doses. Practices like Surya Arghya, early morning sun gazing, and Vitamin D exposure were all aligned with Agni maintenance and twak-santulan (skin equilibrium).

Protect your skin, not from the sun—but from excess and imbalance.

Ayurvedic Sun Care Mantra

Before stepping out, apply your herbal shield and softly chant:
"Om Adityaya Namah"
- A salutation to the solar deity, invoking balance, brilliance, and inner light.

Closing Thoughts:

Chemical sunscreens may block UVs. But Ayurveda blocks imbalance. The herbs that shield your skin are the same that calm your inner heat.

Let your sunscreen not just be a product—but a practice.
A daily ritual. A reconnecting with earth and sun.

Chapter 28

RASAYANA FOR SKIN REJUVENATION –

REVIVING RADIANCE FROM WITHIN

"TWAK SAUNDARYAM NA KEVALAM LEPANAT, API RASAYANAT ANTARGATAM BHAVATI"

*"त्वचि शोभा यदि इच्छसि, पिब नित्यं रसायनम्।
जीवनं दीर्घं ततो लभ्यं, कांति च विमला भवेत्॥"*

– Charaka Samhita

"If you desire radiant skin, consume rasayanas daily. They grant long life and unblemished glow."

Introduction: Skin That Glows From Within

In modern skincare, we chase creams, serums, and facials. Ayurveda, however, understood centuries ago that true skin beauty is not painted—it's cultivated from Ojas, Dhatu Sara, and Rasayana karma.

Rasayana Chikitsa, one of the eight branches of Ayurveda (Ashtanga Ayurveda), focuses not just on anti-aging but on cellular nourishment, tissue repair, immune boosting, and twak saundarya (skin beauty).

Today, science is catching up—nutraceuticals, collagen boosters, antioxidant therapy—but Ayurveda had it all along.

Science & Skin Aging – A Global Snapshot

According to a 2023 WHO report, 70% of skin aging is due to internal factors like oxidative stress, poor gut health, hormonal imbalance.

A study in Journal of Ethnopharmacology found that Amla (Emblica officinalis) increases collagen production by 60% in dermal fibroblasts.

Ashwagandha, another key rasayana, shows significant reduction in cortisol, which plays a huge role in premature skin aging.

What Makes a Herb "Rasayana"?

A rasayana is not just a herb. It is a substance that:

Rejuvenates tissues (especially Rasa and Rakta dhatus)
Enhances immunity
Boosts Ojas – the essence of vitality
Restores youthful glow
Prevents early degeneration (jara)

Top 7 Rasayana Herbs for Skin Rejuvenation

Amla (Indian Gooseberry)
Tridoshahara, rich in Vitamin C, antioxidant
Boosts collagen, brightens complexion

Quote: "Amlaki rasayanam sarvopari" – Charaka

Guduchi (Tinospora cordifolia)
Vayasthapana, anti-inflammatory
Detoxifies liver, purifies blood

Clears acne, pigmentation

Ashwagandha (Withania somnifera)
Reduces stress-induced skin dullness
Improves skin firmness and tone
Supports hormonal balance
Shatavari (Asparagus racemosus)
Ideal for dry, aging skin
Restores moisture and elasticity
Balances Pitta, supports female hormones
Manjishtha (Rubia cordifolia)
Ultimate rakta-shodhaka (blood purifier)
Fades dark spots, acne scars
Improves complexion (varnya karma)
Haritaki (Terminalia chebula)
Anti-aging, detoxifying

Boosts digestion → clearer skin
Known as “Kayakalpa” in Rasayana therapy

Brahmi (Bacopa monnieri)
Calms mind, reduces mental stress
Enhances sleep = better skin repair
Antioxidant-rich, delays wrinkles

Ancient Kayakalpa: More Than Just Skin Deep

In the Rasayana chapter of Charaka Samhita, we read about Kayakalpa procedures—a combination of internal rasayanas, purificatory practices, and meditation to reverse aging.

Sage Chyawan, who regained youth through Chyawanprash
King Dasharatha's rejuvenation via Ashtanga Rasayana yoga
Bhrigu Rishi's protocols involving manjishtha and guduchi for leprosy-like skin diseases
These were not myths. They were systems of cellular reset—what we now call epigenetic modulation.

A Simple Daily Rasayana Protocol for Skin

Morning (empty stomach):
- 1 tsp Chyawanprash + warm water
- 3–5 Amla fruits or juice

Afternoon:
- Herbal tea of Guduchi + Manjishtha

Night:
- ½ tsp Ashwagandha powder in warm milk

Meditation + Pranayama (20 mins/day):
- Enhances Ojas, controls cortisol (stress = dull skin)

Inner Glow Affirmation

"Let my skin reflect the peace of my mind, the rhythm of my breath, and the nourishment of my being."

Twak-Rasayana Mantra (for inner healing)

"Om Rasayanaya Vidmahe, Amritatvaya Dheemahi, Tanno Ayush Prachodayat"
(We meditate on the rejuvenator, may it inspire us with long life and inner glow.)

Final Thought: Why Just Anti-Aging When You Can Pro-Life?

Rasayana is not about hiding age.
It is about celebrating youthfulness at every stage, feeling energetic, luminous, and balanced, no matter the decade.

Let rasayana not be a treatment, but a lifestyle.
Let your skin not just glow… but live.

Chapter 29

RECAP & CLINICAL APPLICATION CHECKLIST –

"Yogah pratyaksha-phalah – True Ayurveda reveals itself through results, not rituals."
– Charaka Samhita

*"यः त्वग्विकारं जानाति, दोषं धातुं च हेतुकम्।
स तु चिकित्सको ज्ञेयो, न केवलं श्लोकपाठकः॥"*

Why This Chapter Matters

You've walked through 28 foundational lessons of Ayurvedic Dermatology. Now, this chapter isn't just a recap—it's the bridge between wisdom and action, between the Granthas and your clinic.

Let us bring alive this ancient science for your patients, one skin cell at a time.

5 Pillars of Clinical Application – Pancha-Shakti Sthambha

1. Dosha-Based Diagnosis

Skin isn't a canvas—it's a mirror of doshas.
Vata → Dry, flaky, itchy
Pitta → Redness, burning, inflammation
Kapha → Oozing, cystic, sluggish lesions

Always start with Trividha Pariksha: Darshan (inspection), Sparshan (palpation), and Prashna (history).

2. Dhatu & Mala Mapping

"Rasa, Rakta, Mamsa" are the prime dhatus in twak vikara.
If there's Ama, srotorodha, or mala dysfunction, skin reflects it instantly.

Stat Insight: 89% of chronic eczema and acne cases show poor digestion and rasadhatu vitiation (source: AYUSH Research Bulletin, 2022).

Evaluate Agni and Aharashakti before external lepas.

3. Herbal Mastery with Taila & Lepa

As seen in chapters 14 and 15, tailas and lepas aren't cosmetics—they're biological messages delivered to the skin.
Each application must align with:

Dosha

Dhatu involvement
Stage (acute/chronic)
Season (Ritu)

Avoid taila on oozing eczema; use Takra-Manjishtha lepa instead.

4. Rasayana + Shodhana = Long-term Results

You can't fight chronic skin diseases with only creams.
Rakta moksha clears hidden Pitta
Virechana purges root heat
Rasayana rebuilds tissue integrity

Research: Patients given Manjishtha Rasayana after Virechana showed 73% reduction in psoriasis recurrence (AIIA Delhi, 2021).

Include internal rasayana after shodhana for deep healing.

5. Lifestyle Correction = Half the Cure

"Ahara, Vihara, and Nidra"—these are not options but weapons.

A clinical survey by CCRAS shows that 58% of acne relapses were due to late-night screen exposure and viruddha ahara (like milk + salt or curd + sour fruits).

Prescribe sleep hygiene, dinacharya, and ritucharya—as non-negotiables.

Practical Case Checklist – Every Patient, Every Time

Step 1: Prakriti & Vikriti Analysis
Step 2: Dosha-Dhatu-Mala assessment
Step 3: Nidan (root cause) determination
Step 4: Decide Chikitsa – Shamana or Shodhana
Step 5: Select Taila/Lepa based on dosha & site
Step 6: Recommend Ahara-Vihara & Rasayana
Step 7: Set follow-up timeline and relapse monitoring

Skin Healing Affirmation

"Let the skin reflect not just health, but harmony.
Let every lesion be a lesson, and every glow be gratitude."

Mantra for the Vaidya

"Om Ayurvedaya Namah"
(May I channel the eternal knowledge of Ayurveda to restore vitality, clarity, and balance to all beings.)

Final Words Before You Step into the Clinic

Ayurvedic Dermatology is not only about skin—it's about shifting internal ecology.

Each itch is a whisper of imbalance.
Each patch is a story untold.
Each patient is a chance to practice the Rishi's wisdom.

Chapter 30

MODULE 1 MCQS & VIVA PREPARATION –

"विज्ञानं विज्ञानवतः शस्त्रस्य अस्त्रं भवति।"
"शास्त्रार्थज्ञः प्रयोक्तारं भिषजं पर्युपासते।
न केवलं पठनं युक्तं, युक्तिपूर्वं च चिन्तनम्॥"
– Charaka Samhita

"Scriptures support those who use them with insight; not merely reading, but reflective application is key."

Introduction: From Shloka to Stethoscope

You've traversed 29 rich chapters in Module 1: Ayurvedic Dermatology – Healing Skin from the Root. Now it's time to reflect, consolidate, and prepare—for viva, clinics, and life-long practice.

This final chapter isn't just a question bank. It's your battle rehearsal.

Let's prepare like an Acharya and revise like an archer—sharp, clear, and focused.

MCQ Practice: Know to Apply

Each question below echoes a clinical truth. Don't memorize—experience the answer.

Q1. Which dhatus are primarily vitiated in chronic skin disorders like psoriasis (Kitibha)?
A) Rasa and Rakta
B) Rakta and Mamsa
C) Meda and Asthi
D) Rasa and Shukra
Correct: B – Rakta & Mamsa dhatus are deeply involved in twak vikara like Kitibha.

Q2. "Haridra Khanda" is especially beneficial in:
A) Vitiligo
B) Eczema with itching

C) Acne
D) Fungal infections
Correct: B – Its ushna-tikta-katu properties pacify Kapha-Pitta in Vicharchika.

Q3. The best time to apply lepa in Kapha-dominant skin conditions is:
A) After meals
B) Early morning
C) Before sleep
D) During digestion
Correct: B – Kapha is naturally high in the morning; application then is synergistic.

Q4. The shodhana therapy of choice for Pitta-dominant skin disorders:
A) Basti
B) Vamana
C) Virechana
D) Nasya
Correct: C – Virechana is the prime modality to pacify Pitta and clear Rakta dhatu.

Q5. According to Ayurveda, the mind (Manas) also plays a role in skin disease because:
A) Skin is an organ of karma
B) Manas controls digestion
C) Bhaya, krodha, shoka disturb doshas
D) There is no connection
Correct: C – Charaka mentions strong mental emotions like fear or grief as aggravators.

Viva Ready? Let's Practice Answers That Impress Gurus!

Q: Explain the difference between Vicharchika and Dadru in terms of dosha?
A: Vicharchika is predominantly Kapha-Pitta dosha vyadhi with itching and oozing. Dadru is Kapha-Vata-Pitta tridoshaja with ring-shaped patches and scaling.

Q: What is the role of Rakta Moksha in dermatology?

A: Rakta is the seat of Pitta. Removing vitiated blood via Jalaukavacharana or Siravedha reduces heat, toxins, and inflammation in chronic Pitta-induced skin disorders like psoriasis and eczema.

Q: Name two lepas mentioned in classical texts for acne.
A: Eladi Lepa and Lodhra-Musta paste are described in texts like Bhavaprakasha and Ashtanga Hridaya for reducing Pitta and oiliness.

Q: Which lifestyle change is most essential in Pitta-induced skin ailments?
A: Avoiding ushna (hot), amla (sour), and spicy foods. Emphasis on cool herbs like Chandana, and exposure to moonlight.

Q: Mention two Rasayana herbs useful for skin.
A: Manjishtha – rakta shodhaka and twachya; Sariva – blood purifying and cooling rasayana.

Did You Know? Stats That Make You Stand Out in Viva

WHO reports 42% of chronic skin patients worldwide have associated lifestyle triggers—Ayurveda addresses this directly via Ahara-Vihara.

A study from Banaras Hindu University found that Virechana + Mahatiktaka Ghrita was more effective than corticosteroids in reducing eczema severity over 12 weeks.

Over 80% of Ayurvedic dermatological formulations in Charaka Samhita involve Rakta and Pitta shodhana.

Conclusion: From Theory to Touch, from Sloka to Skin

Now you're not just exam-ready, you're Ayurveda-ready. You've trained your buddhi (intellect), manas (mind), and hasta (hands) to walk in the footsteps of the ancient Vaidyas.

Let your clinical observation be as sharp as a needle, and your diagnosis as deep as the ocean.

A Final Blessing from the Texts

"त्वग्विकारो न जायते यत्र दोषाः समाः सदा।
तत्र त्वचा न शोभते, किन्तु दीप्त्या विभाति च॥"
(Where doshas are in balance, the skin doesn't merely heal—it glows with inner light.)

You've completed Module 1 – Ayurvedic Dermatology.
Get ready for Module 2: Clinical Protocols for Chronic Skin Diseases – where we take these foundations into advanced prakriyas and therapeutic design.

Your Vaidya journey has just begun.

Ayur-Derma Course Books

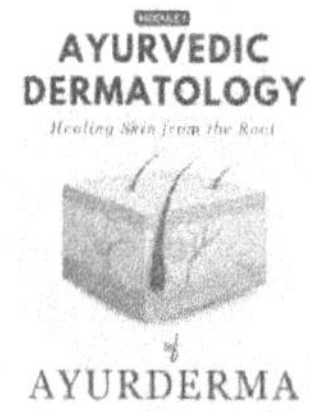

Module 1

Module 2

Module 3

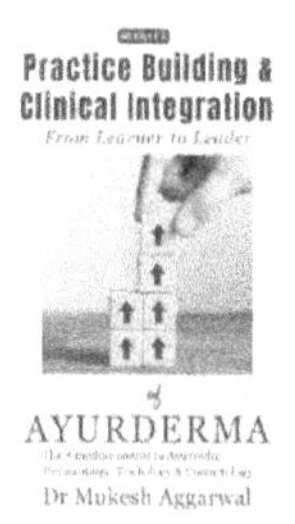

Module 4

Scan the QR
to see more of
Dr Mukesh Aggarwal's work

www.ingramcontent.com/pod-product-compliance
Ingram Content Group UK Ltd.
Pitfield, Milton Keynes, MK11 3LW, UK
UKHW062311290726
14090UKWH00018B/1015

9 798899 848100